The Urbana Free Library

To renew materials call
217-367-4057

BREAKING INTO MAGAZINE WRITING

William Garrett

Published by William Garrett,
PO Box 225201, San Francisco, CA 94122

Copyright © 2002 by William Garrett

ISBN 1-59113-277-0

Printed in the United States of America

Booklocker.com, Inc. 2002

CONTENTS

INTRODUCTION

I've been a freelance writer for 27 years. Over those years, I've gotten many calls from friends (and friends of friends), asking how they, too, can become writers. When I get these calls..."How do you break into writing?"...invariably the conversation comes around to writing for magazines.

Why? Because magazine work is one area of writing that, with no previous writing credits... You've never been published...you have no writing samples... If you can come up with the right idea, and pitch it to the right editor at the right time (when he or she happens to need it), and if you present it well, and correctly... Even if you're a new writer, you can get the assignment.

Did I just make that sound easy? Well it's not quite <u>that</u> easy. Before you can approach an editor, you've got to have something to approach him with. And when you make your approach (your pitch), you have to know what you're doing.

Editors are very busy people. Who are constantly being approached by writers. Many of these writers are approaching these editors wrong. When that happens, a busy editor's busy day gets more complicated. And the easiest thing for editors to do is simply dismiss that writer and his or her wrong approach. Which is exactly what they do. They don't have to tell you what you're doing wrong - they are plenty of writers who are doing it right.

If an editor has a choice of working with two writers she doesn't know, who have proposed equally good ideas... But one writer has done everything right, and the other has done a few things wrong (or one thing wrong...or is - or appears to be - less professional)... Who is that editor going to decide to work with?

So, a very important part of breaking into magazine writing is not only coming up with that all-important idea, but knowing <u>what</u> to do with it and <u>how</u> to do it. And that's what this book is about.

Not how to write the actual article (that's another book), but how to think of something to write about, and how to present your idea, so you'll know what you're doing when you approach a magazine editor with a story proposal, you'll (hopefully) be treated with a little courtesy and respect, and you'll (hopefully) get a response. Even if it's rejection. This book is about the nuts and bolts of breaking into magazine writing.

I'm not promising you'll get rich. I'm not about to reveal 10 Easy Steps or 101 Sure-Fire Secrets to selling your first magazine article and winning a Pulitzer Prize. I am going to give you real, hands-on, practical information, and offer considered advice, from one working writer with almost three decades of experience.

I'm not saying I have all the answers. I'm not saying I do it perfectly, and my way is the only way to do it. I <u>am</u> saying here's what I've learned, and I believe it will help you. It will help you get started as a magazine writer, and it will help you present yourself (and your work) intelligently and professionally. Which in turn will help get you treated better than you might otherwise be treated and, ultimately, help you be professional, or perhaps more professional. At the very least, it will help you avoid many of the mistakes and false starts so many new writers endure before they figure out a better way.

Take what helps you and use it well. Discard what you feel isn't helpful. Use the information in this book to find a better way. And may you publish and prosper.

BEING A NEW WRITER...

If you're reading this book, you're probably a new writer. Or perhaps you're an experienced writer who's new to magazine work. Being a new writer is going to come up a lot in this book, so let's start with this:

There is nothing wrong with being a new writer.

Every writer out there, no matter how successful, was, at one time, a new writer. Every successful anything, was, at one time, a new "that". Picasso was a new painter; Beethoven was a new composer. (All right, maybe it was when they were three years old, but there was a time when one had never painted and the other had never written music.)

So, there is nothing wrong with being a new writer. You might have to explain it, and in some situations it can be a limitation, but you never have to apologize for it.

A FEW OTHER THINGS BEFORE WE BEGIN...

The focus of this book is magazines. But the same things (advice, principles, protocols, etc.) apply to newspapers. What applies to one, applies to the other.

If you decide to approach newspapers, be aware that newspapers generally don't use freelancers to cover news. They do, however, hire freelancers to do feature articles (often for the Sunday edition, or special sections that appear once a week). So if you pitch a story to a newspaper, it should be a feature article, not regular news coverage.

In this book I use the terms "high-end" and "low-end" when referring to magazines. These terms refer to pay rates, not writing quality or content. When I say "high-end" magazine, I mean a publication that pays well. A "low-end" magazine is a publication that doesn't pay very much. (And that's not a value judgment - it's simply a statement of fact.) There can be bad writing in a high-end magazine, and there can be excellent writing in a low-end magazine. It depends on who's doing the writing. And the editing.

For several years I've been teaching classes and workshops on how to break into magazine writing. In putting together this book, I've included many of the questions I've been asked by my students. These questions appear in italics.

GETTING THE IDEA...

I said that if you can come up with the right idea, and pitch it to the right editor at the right time, you can get the assignment. It all starts with an idea.

So, let's have an idea.

But first, let's think about magazines.

What are magazines? They're publications people read to be educated, entertained, and enlightened.

By educated, I mean that people are taught to do something. Anything from how to program a VCR, to how to find a quality budget hotel in New York or London, buy a used piano, or choose the perfect pet for a family of seven living in a studio apartment.

By entertained, I mean...well, entertained. Like reading about a movie star or popular music group...enjoying a memoir about an unforgettable year in Tahiti...laughing at a humor piece.

By enlightened, I mean reading something that presents academic or abstract knowledge. A detailed explanation of the causes of the America Civil War...a biography of Benjamin Franklin...a new take on the Big Bang theory. This is serious reading, to obtain serious knowledge.

Anything that does any one of these (educates, entertains, or enlightens), or any combination of the three, is a potential magazine article.

What are you knowledgeable about?

One of the first rules of writing is: Write what you know. And we all know a lot about at least one thing. Usually it's our job.

Your Job

If someone is paying you to spend all day doing something, you probably know quite a bit about whatever it is you're being paid to do all day. Your job, and the knowledge you have that enables you to do your job, is a potential magazine article. (And if you don't have a job, you know quite a bit about what it's like to <u>not</u> have a job. And <u>that's</u> a potential magazine article.)

Using what you know as the basis of a magazine article isn't limited to your job. Most of us know about other things, too. For instance, our hobbies.

Your Hobby

If you have a hobby, you know quite a bit about whatever your hobby is centered on. And <u>that's</u> a potential magazine article.

I collect film posters. I've written several articles about film posters...which led to writing about fine-art posters...which lead to writing about how to frame and display posters. (Because once you take a poster home, you have to figure out how to frame it. And framing something as large as a poster can cost more than the poster itself. So it helps people to know effective alternative methods of framing and display, and <u>that's</u> a potential magazine article.)

Your Other Interests

What sports do you enjoy? You don't have to be professional. You don't have to be Olympic-quality. You just have to know a lot about some aspect of a sport. Potential magazine article.

Who do you know that's interesting?

They don't have to be famous. Just interesting. Maybe they've successfully come through a medical crisis. Maybe they've done something heroic. Or something unusual. Maybe they have an unusual occupation. Is there anything at all about them that other people might want to read about?

I know someone in the film industry. He's not famous. But he does have an interesting job in an industry that people like to read about. And I've written three articles about him.

You don't have to personally know this interesting person. If you know someone who knows someone interesting...or if you can get access to someone who's interesting... Potential magazine article.

What interesting "something" do you have access to?

If you can get the inside scoop on something that's happening or about to happen... If you can take people behind the scenes of some interesting something... Potential magazine article.

For example, you take daily walks along the river, and every day you pass a large warehouse-type building that's usually locked up. One day you pass it and it's open, and you peer inside and discover that this is where your city keeps old street signs. There's a lot of local history here, and the place itself, and what goes on here, is interesting - and that's a potential magazine article.

What's timely, or about to be timely?

If you're a good trend spotter (fashion, social, political, economic, technological, sexual)... If you see something coming before it gets here... If you're aware of something before it's fully integrated into our culture, before it's part of popular consciousness, or before its significance is perceived, appreciated, or assessed... Potential magazine article.

This happened to me a few months ago. There's a new design element in our culture, something we see on the street every day. Whenever I used to see it, it always registered as "new". ("Ah! There's that, again!") Until one day, when I saw it and no longer had that thought. There was no "There's that, again!" And I realized that this new design element was no longer new. It was changing from being new to passing into our culture and consciousness, becoming integrated into our collective psyche. I'd caught a moment of cultural shift. And that, most certainly, is a potential magazine article.

Travel

Travel writing is a huge market. And if you travel a lot it might be easy for you to break into this market. Because in this case, you're bringing something to the deal.

What you should not do, is call a magazine editor and ask her to send you somewhere so you can write an article for her magazine. I've seen that happen.

Years ago, I was writing for an upscale magazine that published travel articles, and was sitting in my editor's office when the phone rang. The caller asked if the magazine published travel articles. My eminently-genteel editor smiled and said, "Yes."

The caller asked if she was aware that there was a popular festival taking place in the south of France that summer. My always-polite editor smiled again and said, "Yes."

The caller asked if she'd be interested in an article on this popular festival in the south of France. My immaculately-composed editor nodded enthusiastically and said, "Why yes, we would!"

The caller asked if the magazine would send him to France so he could write the article. My impeccably-mannered editor shouted (yes, she raised her voice) "NO!" and hung up on the guy.

Editors don't like to be hustled.

But...let's say you're going to Paris this summer. And let's say there's a festival in Avignon... You could approach a magazine that does travel pieces, and pitch an article on the festival. If it's a good pitch (more about good pitches later), and the right story for that magazine, and the timing is right, you've got a pretty good shot at getting the assignment because you're bringing something to the deal: You're going to be in France anyway, so you're saving the magazine the expense of sending someone there to cover the festival. That's a pretty powerful incentive for an editor to take a shot with a new writer (or a writer she hasn't worked with before).

The magazine won't pay for your trip to Paris. It won't pay for any part of your time in Paris. But (depending on the magazine), it might pay for: your trip to Avignon...your expenses while in Avignon...and your expenses to get back to Paris. And even if they don't pay those expenses, you're getting an assignment and you're getting published.

So, if you think you'd like travel writing, and you're going to do some traveling, do a little research on your destination, find something to write about, and pitch it to a magazine that might publish that story. If it's a good pitch, and the right story, you've got a good chance at getting the assignment.

Publish a few of these, and you're building a reputation as a travel writer. If these pieces are all for the same magazine, you're also building a relationship with that magazine. And, if it's a magazine that sends its writers places (and pays for them to go there), when you become one of "their" writers, they <u>will</u> send you to far-off places and pay for your trip.

What's going on that people want to know about?

People read magazines to be educated, enlightened, or entertained. And anything that does any one of these things, or any combination of these things, is, potentially, a magazine article.

Which means the range of things you can write about is almost limitless.

But...

DON'T WRITE ABOUT SOMETHING
YOU HAVE NO SIMPATICO FOR.
KNOW YOUR LIMITATIONS.

This is so important, it's worth repeating.

DON'T WRITE ABOUT SOMETHING
YOU HAVE NO SIMPATICO FOR.
KNOW YOUR LIMITATIONS.

For each of us, there are things we just don't get. Or we just don't care about. Usually they're topics like nanomolecular biophysics. Or string theory. Might be enology. (And of course there are people who love to write about nanomolecular biophysics. Or string theory. Or enology. Really. But these people might be unable to write about celebrities, home decorating, or their favorite Caribbean island.)

It doesn't matter who we are or what these "I just don't get it" topics are. There are some things we simply have no interest in, or will never be able to understand (no matter how much we study them), or will never be able to write about intelligently (no matter how hard we try).

Know what these are for you. And DO NOT WRITE ABOUT THEM. If you write about something you do not connect with, it will show in the writing - GUARANTEED!

It will not be pretty... It will not be fun... And it could be extremely embarrassing.

On the other hand... Don't be afraid to stretch. If there's an area you don't know, but you can research and learn, definitely consider writing about it.

One of the fascinating (and rewarding) things about magazine writing is that each time you do a piece you become a micro-expert on that topic. Do a couple more, and you become a mini-expert. After a few more, you have Serious Knowledge. A few more, and you're an expert. And once you become known as an expert on a topic, people start coming to you, asking you to write about that subject. Which means you're getting assignments without having to look for them. And that's a position every professional writer wants to be in.

How do I know if my ideas are "big enough"?

They are. No matter what your ideas are.

It doesn't matter how "small" or narrowly focused you might think your idea is. Or how narrowly focused it might in fact <u>be</u>. Your job might be recycling thumbtacks...your hobby might be collecting 13th-century Belgian thimbles...your next travel destination might be Uncle Max's weekly barbecue... Somewhere out there is at least one magazine that might, potentially, be interested.

For example, there's...

Toy Farmer	A magazine about farm toys. (Not just toys... Farm toys.)
Sheep!	For people who raise sheep. (Not ranchers... Not just animals... Sheep.)
Divorce Magazine	For people dealing with separation and divorce.
Mushing	For people involved with dogsledding.
Naturally	For people who enjoy nude recreation.
Vineyard & Winery Management	For grape growers.
The Concrete Producer	For people in the concrete-production industry.

To name only a few... If you're interested in it, or do it, or enjoy reading about it, somewhere out there is probably at least one magazine that publishes stories about it. Which means, somewhere out there is at least one editor who's potentially interested in your idea. You just have to find the magazine. More about that, later.

But first, you've got to <u>have</u> an idea.
So let's have an idea...

You're reading a newspaper, and you come across a story about a small company in Santa Rosa, California, that's involved in a joint venture with General Motors (in Detroit), to make electric cars. And you think, "Hmm, that might make an interesting magazine article."

What types of magazines might, potentially, be interested in this story?

Don't think specific magazines yet - think <u>type</u> of magazine.

Let's talk about that.

In the most general terms, there are two types of magazines: trade magazines and consumer magazines.

Trade magazines are targeted to a specific industry. The stories they print, and the way they're written, are for people in that industry. *Vineyard & Winery Management* is targeted to the grape-growing industry. *The Concrete Producer* is targeted to the concrete-production industry.

Trade magazines assume their readers know the industry, and are reading the magazine to know it better. These magazines are interested in stories, issues, and material that people outside that industry probably won't understand and will very likely find boring. But they're the kind of stories that people in the industry want to read, and need to read, to stay current.

Trade magazines are relatively easy to break in to, but hard to write for. They're hard to write for because in order to write for them you must have an in-depth understanding of the industry the magazine serves. You have to know the history, the issues, the players, the jargon, the trends, and the dynamics of that industry. And most of us don't have this knowledge. Most people who write for trade magazines are people involved in the industry the magazine covers.

Trade magazines are relatively easy to break in to for the same reason. People who have the kind of knowledge required to write for a trade magazine aren't always good writers. So trade-magazine editors are always looking for people who meet both their primary needs: they have the requisite in-depth knowledge of the industry, and they can write.

If you have in-depth knowledge about an industry, and think you'd like to write about that industry (remember, having the knowledge and wanting to write about it are two different things), trade magazines is a market you might consider.

Consumer magazines are what "regular people" read. The magazines you subscribe to or buy every month (unless that includes *Aircraft Maintenance Technology* or *Podiatry Management*) are consumer magazines. And every consumer magazine is targeted to a specific audience.

There are women's magazines (and among these are magazines for younger women, older women, teens, brides, housewives, mothers, working mothers - magazine audiences get very specific)...men's magazines (among these are fashion, adult, adventure, professional, business, leisure)...automotive magazines...entertainment magazines (music, film, games)... science/technology magazines...business magazines (small business/entrepreneurial and big business/corporate)...regional magazines (magazines that focus on a city, county, state)...travel magazines (targeted to high-income, middle-income, budget travelers, alternative travelers, ecotravelers)...etc. etc.

The fact that every magazine has an audience - targets itself to a specific group of people - is an important consideration when deciding what magazines are right for your idea.

Let's go back to our idea - a small company in Santa Rosa, California (in Sonoma County, to be exact), is involved in a joint venture with General Motors (in Detroit), to make electric cars.

What _type_ of magazine might be interested in this idea, or some aspect of this idea?

They don't have to be interested in the whole idea. All it takes to sell an article is generating interest in one aspect of it. And, because most of you won't be writing for trade magazines, let's limit this discussion to consumer magazines.

(In fact, from this point on I'll be referring to consumer magazines. However, just as everything we'll be talking about applies to newspapers as well as magazines, everything we'll be talking about applies to trade magazines, too. Approach trade magazines the same way you'd approach consumer magazines.)

So, what type of magazine might be interested in our idea?

At this point, DON'T LIMIT YOUR THINKING. Just make a list of all the _types_ of magazines that might, potentially, be interested in your idea.

And I mean that literally - make a list. On paper.

When you're breaking into magazine writing (or almost any type of writing), there's a lot of work that needs to be done. Call it legwork, homework, grunt work...call it whatever you want to, as long as you do it. After a while it becomes part of your process, but first you have to train yourself to do it.

I still do all of this work. But now I do it in my head, or I do it automatically, without thinking about it. When I was breaking in, I made that list on paper. And even today, if I find myself not doing something, or not doing it as well or as thoroughly as I should be, I stop, slow down, and do it more carefully.

So, we have an idea about a small company in Santa Rosa that's in a joint venture with GM to make electric cars... What types of magazines might be interested?

Well, lots...but for the purposes of this discussion, let's limit our list to six obvious categories:

Automotive
Because this article deals with cars.

Science/Technology
Because this article deals with an emerging technology.

Regional
Because this article deals with the town of Santa Rosa.

Environmental
Because this article deals with environmental issues.

Big Business/Entrepreneurial
By Big Business, I mean publications like *Barron's*,
The Wall Street Journal, *Forbes*, *Fortune*, *Business Week*,
because there's the General Motors aspect of the story.

By Entrepreneurial, I mean magazines targeted to small
and start-up companies (*Entrepreneur Magazine, Inc.*,
Fortune Small Business, because there's the small-company
part of the story.

Children's
Surprised by this one? It's exactly the kind of thinking you
should be doing at this point. *Highlights for Children,
Cricket, Boys' Life, Girl's Life* would, potentially,
be interested:
"Hey, kids, looks what's out there. It's a car that runs
on batteries. Not the kind of battery that runs your toys,
but a battery big enough to run a car!"
It would be a very different kind of story, and you would
tailor your writing to the age group served by each
magazine... But there could be interest, and at this point
in the process your thinking should be wide open.

You'd write a different article for each type of magazine.

For the automotive magazines, you'd focus on car-specific
elements of the story: the type of car, the chassis, the engine, how
it compares with other cars.

For science/technology magazines, you'd focus on the
technology aspects of the story: the battery, how the battery was
developed, how the battery works, the engine, how the engine
works.

For regionals (in this case, publications targeted to readers and
issues in Santa Rosa, Sonoma County, the San Francisco Bay
Area, or northern California), you'd discuss how this venture will
affect life in Santa Rosa, Sonoma County, the San Francisco Bay
Area, or northern California.

For environmental magazines, you'd examine the benefits of this technology: using less fossil fuels, cleaning up the environment, helping to cut down on the greenhouse effect.

For big-business magazines, you'd zero in on the General Motors aspect of the story. For entrepreneurial magazines, you'd talk about Joe Smith borrowing money from his mother-in-law two years ago and setting up business in the family garage.

For children's magazines, it's "Hey, kids..."

Wait a minute...I don't want to write for automotive magazines.

Don't worry about that yet. After you make your list, you can (and should) think about what types of magazines you <u>don't</u> want to write for.

If you don't want to write for a technology magazine, or an automotive magazine, take it off the list. But don't be afraid to put it on the list to begin with. Because, as I said, at this point you should be open to ideas and possibilities. If you make your list while thinking about what <u>isn't</u> going to be on it, you're thinking is closed instead of open. And if you're closed, you're liable to miss possibilities - like children's magazines.

As you become more familiar with the magazines that are being published, and the markets that are available to you, you won't have to literally make this list because it will be in your head. You'll know the markets and magazines you're comfortable with, and those you prefer to stay away from. But as a new writer, you should be as open as possible. It's easy to cross something off the list. If it's never on your list, because you're not thinking wide enough or imaginatively enough...because you're thinking is narrow instead of open...it's a missed opportunity.

There's another reason to put every possible category on your list. Within a category (say, technology, or business), magazines targeted to a specific field can be geared to different parts of that field. So, while you may not be comfortable writing about high-tech (computers; digital sound), you might be totally at ease writing about basic consumer electronics (televisions; VCRs). Or, while you may not care about Wall Street and annual reports, you might be interested in writing about how Joe Smith started his new business in the family garage.

Don't limit your thinking. You should not venture into areas you're not comfortable writing about. (Know your limitations)... But you should always be open to possibilities. (Don't be afraid to stretch).

OK...you've made your list of the types of magazines that might be interested in this idea. Now take a careful look at it, and eliminate the types of magazines you <u>don't</u> want to write for.

Remember, these aren't specific magazines, they're types of magazines. Categories of magazines. Each category has anywhere from 1 to maybe as many as 12 (or more) publications in it. So if your list has six categories, and you eliminate one or two, you're not eliminating 1/6 or 1/3 of your possible magazines. You're eliminating one or two categories. If there are four categories left, you still have anywhere from 4 to perhaps as many as 48 magazines to pitch. And even if that top number is isn't as high for you (it depends on the types of magazines on your list), you'll still have several magazines to approach.

After you've eliminated the "wrong" (for you) types of magazines, you'll have a list of the "right" (for you) types of magazines for this idea.

Now it's time to choose the specific magazines you want to pitch.

FINDING THE MAGAZINES...

How do you find specific magazines to approach? Again, start with what you know.

What magazines do <u>you</u> read? You're already familiar with these magazines. You know the kinds of articles they publish. Would any of them be interested in this idea?

But of course you're not going to limit yourself to only those publications. As a professional writer, you want to be familiar with all your markets. As a magazine writer, that means knowing what magazines are out there. You don't have to read them all. You just have to know who's out there, and what they're publishing. And, because there's no way you can read them all, you have to know how to research who's out there and what they're publishing.

One way to do this is to frequent newsstands. You'll find magazines that aren't in other research resources, you'll discover magazines you don't know about, and you'll benefit from immediate, hands-on familiarity with any magazine you look at.

This falls under the category of things you do when you're breaking in, and eventually stop doing. When I was breaking in, I spent hours at newsstands (I used to schedule days to do this), looking around to see what was being published. And, while I don't do this for hours any more, I haven't stopped doing it entirely. If I'm meeting someone and I arrive early, or I'm at the airport and have extra time, I still go to a newsstand and look around.

The other way to become (and stay) familiar with what's being published is to read about what's out there and what they're publishing. And that bring us to *Writer's Market.*

Writer's Market is an excellent all-around resource for any freelance writer doing any kind of writing. Magazine writers use it because it has a plethora of information (listings and profiles) about magazines. It doesn't include every magazine out there, and because it's published yearly you'll sometimes find some of its information is out of date... But it lists a lot of magazines, many of which you have no idea exist, and it's the most comprehensive resource I know for finding so many magazines (and information about them) in one place.

You won't learn a magazine's editorial style or see what they've published recently, but you will learn just about everything else you need to know to decide whether or not you might want to write for a particular publication.

Writer's Market costs $29.99 ($49.99 for *Writer's Market Online*, which includes a one-year subscription to WritersMarket.com. That's a savings of $10 (a subscription to WritersMarket.com costs $29.99, without the book) and you'll have access to the online database of markets. The online edition also has listings for newspapers and online markets (which the standard *Writer's Market* does not have).

You can elect not to make the investment, and use the copy at the library, but it's a popular book, so it won't always be available when you want it, and the page you need most is often the one that's been torn out. Also, you'll have to adjust your research schedule to fit library hours. If you're serious about writing for magazines, you should have *Writer's Market* in the house, and always handy.

While we're on the subject of research and resources, another excellent resource is *The Writer*, a monthly trade magazine for writers, that's geared to new writers. Each issue includes a

"Market listings" section that has profiles of magazines (chosen by *The Writer's* editors); "Market news," which provides updates on the publishing industry (very handy: magazines are constantly coming and going, people move around a lot in the publishing industry, and magazines' editorial needs can suddenly change); and notices of writing contests. It also publishes articles about the craft of writing, provides information on the business of writing, and in its pages are answers to questions many new writers have. *The Writer* is available at newsstands ($4.95/issue), or by subscription ($29/year).

Now, let's find some magazines to pitch our idea to.

To do this, we're going to use *Writer's Market.* Remember those magazine categories? Remember your category list? Here's where it all comes together.

Writer's Market lists magazines by category, or genre. If you're naming your genres right (and you will, after you make your first list), you'll find that each genre on your list is in the *Writer's Market* table of contents, organized by the two most general categories: consumer and trade.

Let's say the first category on your list is automotive. Turn to the listings of automotive magazines and carefully read each profile. As you read, make another list. Now you are listing specific magazines.

While reading each profile, think about this: Is this a magazine you can write for? Is this a magazine you want to write for? If it is, put it on your list. If you come across anything that in any way indicates this isn't a magazine for you, move on to the next one.

Let's take a look at some of the information you'll find in a *Writer's Market* magazine profile.

The first section:

<u>The name and address</u> of the magazine.

<u>A phone number</u>. Which you should not call - editors don't want phone calls from writers they don't know. Never approach an editor you don't know by phone. Always contact them in writing. And always include an **SASE** (Self-Addressed Stamped envelope). More about that later. There's also an <u>e-mail address</u> and a <u>Web site address</u>.

<u>A contact name</u>. The is the person to whom you should send your query letter. (More about that later, too.)

<u>How much of the magazine's content is freelance written</u>. Obviously, the higher the percentage of freelance content, the better your odds of selling an idea to the magazine. Which isn't to say that if a magazine is only 10% freelance written you don't stand a chance. But it does indicate that the magazine might be harder to sell to than a magazine that's 90% freelance written.

<u>A general statement about the magazine</u>. Who reads it, and/or what its goal is, and/or how it sees itself. This is usually a quotation from someone at the magazine, and might provide a little insight into how that magazine will respond to your idea.

<u>The magazine's payment policy</u>. (More about this later.)

<u>What rights the magazine buys</u>. (More about this later, too.)

Editorial lead time. The **lead time** is how far ahead of its publication date a magazine works. This isn't a particularly crucial thing to know unless your idea is somehow pegged to the calendar or a season. If you have a Halloween-related idea, and a magazine's lead time is, say, three months, the editor will want to assign the story (at least) three months before the October issue is due to hit the stands (which will usually be in September). Because you'll need time to write the story (and the editor needs time to consider your proposal), pitch that magazine your Halloween-related idea in early April. (Or earlier, so you'll have time to send the idea to more than one magazine, if necessary.)

If your idea is not time sensitive, lead time is generally not a major consideration.

Submission policy. This is how the magazine wants writers to submit ideas. Some magazines prefer regular mail. Some prefer e-mail. Some will accept either. (More about this later.)

Response time. This is how long it takes the magazine to respond to a query. (A lot more about this later.)

Sample copy. This tells you how you can get a sample copy of the magazine. (More later.)

Writer's guidelines. **Writer's guidelines** are information sheets put out by magazines, that provide the essential information you need to help you decide if a particular magazine is right for your idea (and you). Often it's the same information you'll find in *Writer's Market*, but some writers like to have both, in case one has information the other doesn't. (And, because *Writer's Market* is published yearly, a magazine's writer's guidelines might be more up-to-date.)

The second section (Nonfiction):

The type of material the magazine is interested in. Sometimes this is simply a list, sometimes it's another quotation from someone at the magazine. Sometimes it includes what the magazine doesn't want. Pay attention to this - it can save you a lot of time and energy. (And even if your idea isn't the type of material the magazine doesn't want, be sure it's included in the material it does want.)

How many manuscripts (mss) the magazine buys a year. Like a magazine's percentage of freelance writing, this is an indication of how open the magazine is to outside submissions, and what your chances are of selling your idea to this publication. The higher the number of manuscripts a magazine buys, the better your odds that yours might be one of them.

Clips. **Clips** are writing samples. If a magazine says to query with published clips, it wants you to include writing samples with your query letter. (More about that later.)

Length. This is the **word count**. It tells you how long an article (in words) the magazine will likely want. The standard formula for word count is 250 words per page, double-spaced. If a magazine's profile says, "Length: 1,500-2,800 words," and you get a feature assignment from this magazine, you'll be expected to give them anywhere from 1500 words (6 pages) to 2800 words (12 pages). (This a ballpark figure. An editor can assign a shorter (or longer) feature.) If you find yourself thinking, "My goodness, I could never write even 6 pages on this topic, then perhaps this isn't a magazine for you. If you feel you can write 6-12 pages on your topic, perhaps this is a magazine for you.

Pays. What the magazine pays. Which means it's time to talk about money. And the most important thing to say about money is:

FOR A NEW WRITER, MONEY IS SECONDARY.

Yes, it's nice to get paid to write...and yes, you want to get to write...and yes, you should get paid to write. But...

FOR A NEW WRITER,
THE MOST IMPORTANT THING IS TO GET PUBLISHED.

I have a former student who's been published eight times in one magazine. Pretty good. And for all this work she received... Not one penny. She did it all for free. But nobody knows that. All anyone knows is, she has eight clips. All anyone sees when they look at her resume is that she's been published eight times in one magazine. Which means that an editor saw her writing and liked it enough to publish it. Eight times. And that is pretty good!

No one knows how much you get paid for an article. And very few people ask, except, perhaps, friends who are curious, and other writers. Editors will not ask what you've been paid (it does happen, but not often), and the fact that you've been published has far more impact than the fact that you were paid little, very little, or nothing, when you were.

When you tell people you're a writer, the first question is almost always, "Where have you been published?" (Or "Have I read anything you've written?" Which is the same thing.) Look at the difference between having to say "Well, I haven't been published yet," and being able to say, "Well, I just had a piece published last month."

Oh, you're a published writer.

So, for the new writer, money is secondary. The important thing is to be able to say you've been published. And, if you're talking to an editor, to be able to say you have writing samples.

While we're on the subject of money, and how much (or how little) you might be paid... It's easier to break in with lower-paying magazines than higher-paying magazines. Editors at high-end magazines generally prefer to work with experienced writers. Writers who understand the needs of the magazine, know what the editor wants, give the editor what she wants, and require minimal editing after the piece is turned in. That's why they pay the big bucks. (That doesn't mean that as a new writer you <u>can't</u> get published in a high-end magazine. Remember, if you pitch the right idea at the right time... So if you're comfortable pitching the big guys, go ahead. If the very fact that they <u>are</u> big guys is intimidating, wait until you're comfortable with this before you pitch them.)

Editors at low-end magazines know they attract new writers, and are generally more open to working with new writers. Also, editors at low-end magazines are often willing to do more hand-holding, and help you develop your piece so it meets their requirements. (And of course an editor at a low-end magazine can be extremely demanding. Just as an editor at a high-end national can be a total sweetheart.)

I'm often asked if getting published in small, low-end magazines hurts your chances of being published in high-end magazines. Don't be concerned about that. Just because you're working for a low-paying magazine this month, doesn't mean that next month you won't be working for a high-paying glossy national. An editor at a high-end national publication isn't going to refuse to give you an assignment simply because so far you've worked "only" with the "little guys." In fact, he'd rather you've been published <u>somewhere</u>, than not at all.

A friend of mine had her first piece published in a small, local, free weekly. Next time out, she got an assignment from her city's most prestigious newspaper. (Which, by the way, didn't pay any more than the free weekly. Newspapers pay less than magazines. They have to - they chew up a huge amount of material.)

So don't worry about how much you're getting paid or where you're being published. Just get published. Hopefully, the big names, and the higher-paying assignments, will come in their own time. (And yes, we'll discuss money in more detail later.)

Back to the *Writer's Market* magazine profile, and the last piece of information in the Nonfiction section.

<u>Expenses</u>. Some magazines pay the expenses of a writer on assignment. Some don't. (More about that later.)

The third section (Photos):

This section doesn't appear in every magazine profile. We'll discuss why later.

The fourth section (Columns/Departments):

This, too, doesn't appear in every profile. When it does, look at it carefully. Some magazines have specialized sections that focus on specific topics (entertainment, technology, fashion, science, cooking, etc.). These sections are often short articles, and very often they're an easier way to break into a magazine. An editor might think twice about assigning a feature article to a new writer, but she might be willing to take a shot with a new writer to whom she can assign a shorter piece. So, if you are a new writer, or you're trying to break into a hard-to-get magazine, you might think about pitching an idea for one of the magazine's special sections, rather than a feature. It'll pay less, but your chances of getting published are better. And money is secondary.

Last section (Tips):

Tips are not in every profile. When they are, they're usually another quotation from someone at the magazine, giving additional information and/or Do's and Don'ts. This information can be very helpful. You're getting an insider's advice. Sort of like having a cousin at the magazine.

If, after reading a magazine's entire profile, you feel you can write for this magazine, put it on your list.

I make an "A" list and a "B" list.

My "A" list titles are the magazines I really want to do this article for. My "B" list titles are the "maybes" - magazines I'm willing to do this article for, but there's something in the profile that's making me think twice.

The two factors that determine my "A" list and "B" list are money and prestige.

You said money is secondary.

It is. But as an established, professional writer, I don't seek out assignments that don't adequately compensate me for my time and energy. If I'm looking for an assignment, I'm going to seek out a well-paying assignment.

Now, having said that, I'll say this: Everything is situational. And when prestige enters the picture, money exits through the nearest door. (Or window.) A publication that doesn't pay a lot, but offers prestige (like *The New York Times* or the *San Francisco Chronicle*), immediately goes on my "A" list. It's a trade-off: I'm giving up the big bucks for the big name. Because I have a lot to gain from being able to put that name on my resume.

So why do I make a "B" list at all? Because after I'm rejected by all the magazines on my "A" list (and you will get rejected a lot), those "B's" starting looking good!

I'm not sure a new writer should have an "A" list and a "B" list (with one exception, that I'll get to later). Because...the point is to get published.

With this in mind, any magazine is worth trying for. But you'll have to work with these people. And you'll have to work with them on their terms - according to the magazine's guidelines, policies, and editorial approach to its content. So if anything in the profile makes you uncomfortable, move on to another magazine.

And...

DON'T WRITE FOR A MAGAZINE YOU DON'T CONNECT WITH.

This is something else that's so important it's worth repeating.

DON'T WRITE FOR A MAGAZINE
YOU DON'T CONNECT WITH.

Every magazine has a **voice**. An editorial style. As a writer for that magazine, you have to use that voice. If you think a magazine is sexist, or stupid, or politically incorrect... If you have any problem at all, on any level whatsoever, with a magazine... Don't even attempt to write for it.

Because you will have to write in their voice. You will have to write sexist, or stupid, or politically incorrect. If you don't, they might reject your work. Or - what could be worse - they will accept your work. And they will change it to match their sexist, stupid, politically-incorrect voice. And they will publish it under your name. They can do this...and they will do this, without a second thought.

So don't pitch a magazine you don't connect with. Don't pitch a magazine you feel you can't write for. Don't pitch a magazine you're not comfortable writing for. Don't pitch a magazine in which you don't want to see your name.

What is going on your list of magazines are the publications you want to do this article for. When you finish one category from your magazine genre list, go on to the next category, read the profiles, and add more magazines to your titles list. And organize your titles list by category. (You'll see why, later.)

After you've gone through all the genres on your category list, you have a list of the magazines you're going to pitch this idea to.

So...you have an idea...you know the types of magazines that might be interested in this idea...you have a list of specific magazines you want to write this article for... Now it's time to write the article. Right?

Nope. It's time to write the query letter.

THE QUERY LETTER...
(Overview)

That's Query Letter, <u>not</u> article.

DON'T WRITE THE ARTICLE
UNTIL YOU HAVE THE ASSIGNMENT.

Because...
1) Editors don't want unsolicited manuscripts.

The last thing a busy editor wants, is to open an envelope from a writer she doesn't know, and watch a manuscript she didn't ask for, drop onto her desk.

Many magazines will not accept unsolicited manuscripts. Many editors will not read them. Many editors will, literally, throw them away.

Why don't editors want unsolicited manuscripts?
Maybe one of them is the magazine's next great article.

Maybe. But unsolicited manuscripts can lead to more problems than potential articles.

The most common problem (or potential problem) is, the idea has already been assigned to another writer.

When we get an idea, we tend to think we're the only one in the world who has that idea. But the very fact that you've thought of it shows that it's thinkable. Which means it's possible that another writer (or editor) on the other side of the country has thought of it, too. Which means it's possible that the magazine is already working on "your" story. Now you submit your manuscript (which the magazine has not asked for), and which the editor is going to reject because it's already been assigned, you get rejected, two months later the magazine comes out with the story, and you're screaming rip-off.

You weren't ripped off. You were late. (You should have approached the magazine sooner.) This is one big reason magazine editors don't read unsolicited manuscripts.

Another reason editors don't want to deal with unsolicited manuscripts is they simply don't have the time. They're busy assigning stories, reading articles they did ask for, meeting with writers, other editors, and graphics people, keeping track of stories they've assigned, and doing a thousand other things. Looking at a story they haven't asked for takes time and energy away from all these things.

2) You don't know how long the piece should be.

When you get an assignment, the editor will tell you how long an article he wants - your word count. These aren't random numbers editors pull out of the air. They're based on how much space the magazine can or wants to devote to that article. You may think your idea deserves 3,000 words, but it might work better for a particular magazine at 2,000 words. And "fixing" the piece won't be just a matter of lopping off 1,000 words. The number of words you write affects and determines your article's structure. So plunging ahead and writing the article without first discussing word count with an editor can result in your producing a piece that's better suited to your needs than the magazine's.

3) You don't know what focus the magazine may want.

When an editor assigns an article, she may want you to focus on a particular aspect or element of the story. She may want to zero in on something you glanced over in your query. Or there might be a story element she does not want to emphasize, or cover at all. If you don't talk to the editor before you write the article, you won't know her thinking on the best way to do this story for her magazine.

4) You don't know what voice to write in.

Well, yes, you do, if you've done your homework, read the magazine you're sending the article to, and studied its voice. But let's say you do all that, and your unsolicited manuscript is rejected. What do you do then?

Every magazine has a voice. And they are not interchangeable. Not even among magazines in the same category. Every woman's magazine does not sound like every other woman's magazine.

You can write the "perfect" article, but if it's not in the voice of the magazine you send it to, it's not going to feel right to the editor. And most editors are not going to make the effort to tell you how to rework your unsolicited article so it does feel right to them. It's easier for them to simply reject it.

You can't write a generic article (say, for men's publications) and send it to every magazine in that category. (It won't be right for all the magazines whose voice it doesn't match.) If you write a generic article and send it to one men's magazine, and it's rejected, you can't simply it to another men's magazine. There is no generic voice for all men's magazines. Every magazine has its own voice.

You could recast the article so it is in the second magazine's voice... But if it's rejected by that magazine, you have to rewrite it before you can send it to a third magazine. Do you know how much time this is taking? Professional writers don't work this way.

Which brings us to yet another reason not to write the article before you have the assignment.

5) Professional writers try not to write unless they know they're getting paid, and know how much they're being paid. Writing "for free" is called writing **on speculation** or "on spec".

But you said money is secondary.

It is. But at some point you should start thinking like a professional. Consider this practice.

So...you don't write the article until you get the assignment.

WITH THESE EXCEPTIONS:

Personal Essays

Op-ed pieces

Humor

Magazines that publish these types of pieces do want the article, unasked for. Because these types of writing are too subjective to be judged from a query letter.

Personal essays are pieces written about your experiences or expressing your thoughts. You can't query an editor and say, "I have lots of experiences, and thoughts about them, to share. Pay me, and I'll share my thoughts." He has to see what those experiences or thoughts are, and how you express them on the page.

Op-ed (opposite-editorial) pieces are like personal essays, but focus on thoughts (as opposed to experiences) and address a current issue. You can't approach an editor and say, "I have a lot of thoughts and opinions about global warming and what can be done about it. Pay me and I'll write down my thoughts." The editor has to see what you're going to say, and how you're going to say it, before he can decide whether or not he wants to publish it.

(By the way, op-ed pieces are usually written by famous people or someone prominent in a field related to the issue. If you want to try this kind of writing, and aren't famous or prominent in a field, you might be better off with personal essays instead of op-ed pieces. On the other hand, if you have a good op-ed piece in mind, go for it. The worst that can happen is you'll get rejected. Meanwhile, you're writing, and that will help you be a better writer. And what if you <u>don't</u> get rejected?)

As for humor, simply telling someone you're funny doesn't do it - humor is too subjective. An editor has to see for herself whether you're funny or not, and if your humor is the type of humor her magazine publishes.

So, if you write personal essays, op-ed pieces, or humor pieces, you do write them on spec, and you do send the magazine an unsolicited manuscript. These editors not only look at unsolicited manuscripts - they insist on them.

And there will be times when you're <u>told</u> by an editor to write the piece on spec. This might happen because it's the magazine's policy that all articles are written on spec. Or the magazine has a policy that articles by new writers are done on spec. Or because the editor isn't sure about the idea (or you) and wants to see the article before agreeing to publish it. These are entirely different situations.

When you pitch a story to an editor and you're told to go ahead and write the article, but it's on speculation, you're getting an assignment. There's no guarantee they'll publish the article - that's why you're being told to write it on spec - but the magazine is expressing interest, you have the assignment, and the editor will tell you what you'll need to know to write the article she wants.

Yes, you are doing the article on spec, but it's the only way you'll get the assignment (which doesn't make it any more appealing to a professional writer)... And yes, you'll be submitting a spec manuscript, but it won't be an unsolicited manuscript. The editor has asked for it, and of course will read it.

A few more Do's and Don'ts about pitching...

NEVER PHONE A MAGAZINE EDITOR YOU DON'T KNOW, TO PITCH AN IDEA.

They don't like this. They're busy. It's not the way to do it.

I know someone who called an editor she didn't know,
pitched a story on the phone, was told to write
a query letter, and then was asked to do the article.

And there are people who sell their first screenplay for $1,000,000. And writers who commit suicide because they've written 27 books that never got published. It's called luck. Stuff happens. The permutations of a situation are endless.

For every person who breaks the rules and has wonderful things happen, there are countless people who break the rules and pay the price. That's called bad luck.

I know someone who called an editor she didn't know and had a lovely conversation. But she never did sell that article.

I break my share of rules. Sometimes it works out for me. Sometimes it doesn't. In the end, it comes down to doing what you're comfortable with.

But, one rule I never break is:

NEVER PHONE A MAGAZINE EDITOR
YOU DON'T KNOW, TO PITCH AN IDEA

Another rule you should never break is:

BEFORE YOU PITCH ANY MAGAZINE,
BECOME FAMILIAR WITH IT.

Read an issue or two. Become familiar with what they're publishing, and learn the magazine's voice. Be sure it's a magazine you can, and want to, write for.

This is non-negotiable. And if you think you don't have to do it, consider the alternative: You pitch a magazine you've never looked at...you get the assignment...and then you discover that for some reason (might be the voice, might be the level of writing, might be the magazine's agenda, might be anything at all) you can't write for that magazine.

This isn't going to end happily. You owe the editor a story. You'll either have to find a way to get out of doing the story (in which case you haven't lived up to your end of the deal, and why would this editor ever work with you again)... Or you'll write a bad article (in which case why would this editor ever work with you again). And the entire situation could have been avoided if only you'd taken the time to make yourself familiar with the magazine before you pitched it.

The best way to become familiar with a magazine is, as I've said, to read a couple of issues (at the newsstand, at the library). Or send for a sample copy of the magazine. (That's why *Writer's Market* profiles include information about getting sample copies.)

Another way to learn about a magazine is to study its writer's guidelines. (Remember those, from *Writer's Market*?) You can get a magazine's guidelines by writing a letter to the magazine and asking for their writer's guidelines. (Include an SASE). However, writer's guidelines take a while to arrive. If your story is time-sensitive, you may not have time to send for them.

One strategy: If you know there's a magazine you may want to write for some day, send for their guidelines now, when time isn't a factor.

You can also get a magazine's guidelines online, if the publication has a Web site or if its guidelines are posted on another site. *Writer's Market* includes a magazine's Web site in its profile, and the Resources section of this book lists some Web sites that provide writer's guidelines.

The obvious advantage to getting writer's guidelines online is it's faster than sending for them by mail. It's also cheaper. (If you send for a lot of guidelines, all that postage (two stamps per request) begins to add up.

When you get a magazine's guidelines online, always try to get them directly from that publication's Web site. Getting guidelines from other Web sites can sometimes be problematic. The infor-mation on some sites isn't as comprehensive or complete as the magazine's Web site or *Writer's Market*. Some sites want you to buy their service or newsletter or special report. Sometimes they have sample listings, or partial listings, and tell you that you'll get the entire listing (or access to all the listings) when you buy their service or newsletter or special report.

Remember, writer's guidelines will <u>not</u> make you familiar with a magazine's voice (or what articles it's recently published). To <u>really</u> know a magazine, you have to read it.

Once you're familiar with the magazine(s) you want to approach, it's time to write the query letter.

THE QUERY LETTER...
(Specifics)

The following letters (with one exception) are actual query letters (all names and addresses have been changed). With that one exception, they were all successful. They're provided here as models, and to be used as a basis for illustration and discussion. I am by no means saying this is the only way to write a query letter, or that every query letter should sound like these. Feel free to take and use what works for you, or simply use these letters as a jumping-off point, and go from there. This is what has worked for these writers. Do what works for you.

However, there are reasons why these letters worked. So as you read the following discussion, think about the dynamics behind each letter. Discard what you want to, but be sure you replace it with something. And make it something that's equally good.

Before you read Letter #1, simply look at it. Don't read it... Just look at it.

What do you notice?

It's short.

Query letters are short. The ideal length is one page. The world certainly won't come to an end if you write a two-page query letter, but never go over two pages.

Editors are very busy people. They get anywhere from dozens to hundreds of queries a month. Give them a reason not to read yours (and simply not being in the mood to read a three-page letter is reason enough), and they won't. So don't give them any reasons not to read your letter.

One purpose of the query is to tell the editor about the article you want to write for her magazine, and give her a sense of how you intend to write it. If you can't present your basic idea and intent directly and succinctly, what kind of article are you liable to turn in?

OK, now read Letter #1.

LETTER # 1

1234 Main St.
San Francisco, CA 94123
May 10, 1980

Donna Riston
Redbook
567 6th Avenue
New York, NY 10036

Ms. Riston:

I'm writing to suggest an article for *Redbook* on framing and display.

While everyone knows how much a framed piece enhances a room, few people are aware of the less-expensive alternative display methods available, such as wet mounting, museum mounting, and shrink wrapping. There are also devices like the vacuum press, which takes the wrinkles out of paper during mounting, making it possible to create a handsome display of old or crumpled paper.

What I have in mind is a combination "how-to"/"complete guide" type of piece, which I think would be of great interest to your readers, and is particularly timely in terms of today's money crunch. (A large poster might cost as much as $100 to frame under glass; other methods provide a beautiful setting for as little as $20.)

My magazine credits include articles for *McCall's*, the *Washington Post*, *American Film*, and *Northwest Orient*, among other publications.

I look forward to hearing from you and can be reached at the above address or at (415) 123-4567.

Sincerely,

Mike Brautler

LETTER #1

Let's start with the salutation. This letter is addressed to a specific person, not "Editor". Unless you're specifically directed to (by the magazine, the writer's guidelines), always address your query letter to a specific person.

How do you find out who this person is? *Writer's Market* and magazines' guidelines list editors' names. You can also get this information at a magazine's Web site.

If you're pitching a magazine that's not listed in *Writer's Market* (or you think the name listed there might no longer be current), or you don't have the magazine's guidelines, or the magazine does not have a Web site, you can always get an editor's name from the magazine's masthead.

Every magazine has a **masthead** - a list of the magazine's staff. The masthead is at the front of the magazine, among the first 10 pages.

Every masthead is different, and they do not all list the same positions. Typical positions are Publisher, Managing Editor, Editor, Editor-in-Chief, Senior Editor, and Associate Editor.

Generally, send your query to the Managing Editor or Editor (or Senior Editor). Not the Publisher. If you have a choice between two editors, and one is a woman, and the other is a man, and you think your article might have more appeal to a man, contact the man; if you think your article might have more appeal to a woman, contact the woman.

If a magazine lists different editors for specific sections (Features Editor, Technology Editor, Entertainment Editor), and your article falls into one of these categories, send your query to that editor.

Paragraph 1:

Gets right to the point. A query letter is a business letter, not a social occasion.

The first sentence of this letter...the entire first paragraph... states simply and clearly why Mike is contacting this editor. Why is this editor reading this letter from this writer she doesn't know? Because he has an idea for her magazine: an article on framing and display.

Being businesslike, direct, and concise does two things. It immediately tells the editor what this communication is about. If she's interested in the idea, she'll keep reading. If she isn't, she'll put the letter aside and go on to the next query.

It also begins to establish Mike's credibility. Because it shows the editor he's a writer who knows (and respects) how precious her time is. It communicates: "I know you're busy, so I'll get right to the point. You can trust me. I'm not going to waste your time." This, in turn, encourages the editor to take Mike seriously and treat his query with professional respect.

If you send an editor a query letter with a long rambling beginning that doesn't communicate well and makes her work harder than she already is, you're sending the message that you're a writer who is likely to waste her time (or at least take up more of her time than she's comfortable giving). You're a writer who's going to be "work." If I'm a busy editor, would I rather work with a writer who's going to be work, or a writer I believe will make my life easier?

Paragraph 2:

Demonstrates the writer's knowledge of the topic.
This is extremely important. Why should this editor hire this writer to do this piece? Because Mike knows this subject. He's done his homework, and is qualified to write about this topic.

Paragraph 3:

Describes the type of article the writer wants to write, and indicates why it's relevant to the magazine's readers.
In this case, it also shows that Mike is familiar with the magazine. How does he know they publish "how-to"/"complete guide" pieces? He's read the magazine. And why bother to let the editor know that? This also helps establish Mike's credibility. It communicates that he's looked at the magazine, thought about the type of articles it publishes (which shows he does his homework and is serious about his craft) and, having done that, <u>still</u> feels the article is right for the magazine. He's not just shotgunning this query all over town. He's thinking about what he's doing. Which is another reason for the editor to take him seriously as a potential contributor to her magazine, and feel he's a writer she might want to work with.

Paragraph 4:

Very Important Paragraph. This paragraph establishes your credibility as a writer.
Mike has been published in at least four magazines. He must be doing something right.

But I'm a new writer. I don't have any credits.
What do I do?

If you don't have magazine credits, what else do you have? Have you been published anywhere else? Any other writing credits? Any other writing experience?

Magazine experience is best because it's the most relevant. But if you've never been published in a magazine, think about where else you <u>have</u> been published.

This includes:
Articles you've written for newsletters
Material you've had published on the Internet
Brochures or press releases you've written
Books you've published yourself (self-publishing)
Chapters of books you've written
Articles in your college newspaper

It does not include:
Letters to the editor
Articles you've written for your high school paper
(Unless you've graduated from high school within the last two years)

A quick word about the Internet...

It has not yet achieved the credibility or legitimacy that print journalism enjoys. One reason for this is that anyone can publish anything on the Internet. Another reason is, often the level of editing and vetting of information isn't as high on the Internet as it is in print. And even when it is, mistakes can occur because of technology glitches. (Of course, there are extremely reputable Web sites, and more are being created all the time. But, in general, print (especially print journalism), is regarded as a "purer", more "legitimate" medium than the Internet.)

However, being published on the Internet is still being published. So if you have been published on the Internet (and your writing hasn't appeared in print, or you have only one or two print credits), by all means include this in your credibility paragraph (with the name of the Web site). And if you're pitching a Web magazine, <u>definitely</u> include it. It may help you more than being published in print, because it's more relevant.

If you've <u>never</u> been published, do you have job-related writing experience?

I had one student who'd never been published, but whose job included writing manuals for his company. In the credibility paragraph, he'd write something like: "My experience includes writing company manuals [or you could say corporate communications] as part of my job with the ABC corporation for the last five years."

No, it's not magazine work, but it does show that he has some experience writing. And he's held the job for five years, so he must be somewhat good at it.

If you have no job-related writing experience, do you have any relevant professional experience?

A friend of mine manages a framing store. He's not a writer, but he sure knows a lot about framing and display. In his credibility paragraph, he would write something like: "As the manager of You've Been Framed for the last seven years, I am intimately familiar with all aspects of framing and display."

In this case, his professional expertise makes up (to some degree) for his lack of writing expertise. Of course the editor would prefer an experienced writer, but if the query letter is written well (more about that later), this could make the difference. He's still a better candidate for the assignment than someone who's never been published and has no background in framing and display.

Do you have any relevant educational experience?
A woman in one workshop I taught wanted to pitch an article in the area in which she'd written her Ph.D. dissertation. She would write something like: "Having earned my Ph.D. with a dissertation on this topic, I've done exhaustive research in this area and have stayed current with it since leaving school."

Again, she's not an experienced writer, but she clearly knows the topic, she's written a book-length manuscript on it, and what she wrote was good enough to get her the Ph.D. Which certainly makes her qualified to write on this subject, and a better candidate for the assignment than someone who's never been published and hasn't done such in-depth research.

Don't have any of this? What else do you have? Is there anything in your life or background that makes you the right person to do this piece?
In one workshop, a woman wanted to write an article about a certain childhood illness. She'd never been published and had no writing experience at all. But she did have three children.

She would write something like: "As the mother of three, I've spent many nights comforting a sick child, and know all-too-well what every parent goes through when one of their children is ill."

She's not an experienced writer, but she's a better candidate than the new writer who's never been in the situation.

The purpose of the credibility paragraph is to establish your suitability to do this piece for this magazine. Anything that puts you over as the person they should hire goes in this paragraph.

Writing experience is best. Lacking that, include anything else that will make you look good.

If you have <u>absolutely</u> <u>nothing</u> you can say...if there is nothing in your background that you can put in this paragraph... Leave it out. You don't have to tell them you have no writing experience whatsoever. They'll figure that out on their own.

One more thing about the credibility paragraph...

NEVER LIE ABOUT YOUR CREDENTIALS
OR EXPERIENCE.

Editors may or may not ask for writing samples. But you never know if or when they will. And if I'm an editor, and you're a writer who wants to work for my magazine, and I ask for samples, and you don't have them, and I discover you're lying to me... There goes the relationship. We don't even know each other, and you're lying to me? Why in the world would I ever want to work with you?

And it doesn't matter that I'm "only" the editor at a local weekly with a circulation of five. People move around a lot in publishing. Next year I might be the editor at *Woman's Day*. Or *Vanity Fair*. And <u>yours</u> will be the name I happen to remember.

If you have writing samples that you've published under a different name, that's OK.

If you didn't get a byline, but you wrote it, that's OK.

If you wrote it a long time ago, and no longer have a copy, that's OK.

But if you haven't written it, don't say you did. Don't lie. It's dishonest, it's unprofessional, it's bad karma.

<u>NEVER</u> SAY YOU'VE WRITTEN SOMETHING
THAT YOU HAVEN'T WRITTEN.

Paragraph 5:

Does two things. It ends the letter on a warm hopeful note, and includes a phone number.

Always include your phone number. What could be more frustrating than for an editor to want to give you the assignment, and not be able to reach you?

If you use letterhead stationery, your phone number will be part of your letterhead and does not have to be repeated here.

Two more things about this letter...

1) It has no mistakes.

YOUR QUERY LETTER MUST BE
ABSOLUTELY ERROR-FREE.

Assuming you're working on a computer, run the letter through your spell check, run it through your grammar check, proofread it, then run it through your spell check and grammar check again. Then print it, proofread it, and run it through your spell check and grammar check one more time. I'm serious about that.

A letter with mistakes communicates a message:
You don't know how to write.
You don't know grammar, spelling, or punctuation.
You do know grammar, spelling, or punctuation, but you're careless.
You know grammar, spelling, and punctuation, and you saw the errors, but you didn't care enough to correct them
You're unprofessional.

All of these messages are bad. Any <u>one</u> of these messages is bad. Regardless of which one (or ones) the editor settles on... Regardless of whether you happen to think it's (they're) true... This is what the editor thinks. And why would an editor choose to work with a writer who is any one of the above?

Also, if you can't write a one-page letter free of errors, why in the world would an editor trust you with an entire article?

I said to proofread your letter on paper as well as on the screen, because the eye sees things differently on paper. I'm always amazed that, after 27 years, I will still catch errors on paper that I've missed on the screen. So after you're convinced that the letter on your computer screen is perfect, print it out and read it again, on paper.

If you find errors, don't correct them by hand - no matter how small they are. Correct them on the screen and reprint the letter. I'm serious about that, too.

NEVER SEND A LETTER WITH HAND-WRITTEN CORRECTIONS.

Editors will send them to us, but we can <u>not</u> send one to them.

There was a time when you could. Back in the precomputer days, everyone was working on typewriters. And after typing an error-free page, we'd almost always make a mistake in the last paragraph. Or the last line. The only solution was to retype the entire letter, which no one wanted to do, so everyone was sending out letters with mistakes they'd found and corrected by hand.

Computers have changed that. Computers have raised the standards. You no longer have to retype an entire page - just go back to the screen, correct the mistake, and print out a new letter.

Because the standards are now higher, and these higher standards are within everyone's reach, when you fail to meet them, it stands out as Very Big.

One little hand correction will not bring civilization as we know it to an end. But because your letter might be the only one with such a correction (or if not the only one, maybe one in ten), you're the one who appears to be less professional than the others (or the other nine). If I'm an editor, and I have a choice of 10 writers, why would I go with the one whom I believe (rightly or wrongly) is the least (or even a little less) professional?

You're the one who wants the assignment. It's up to you to convince the editor that you're the one to give it to.

Sound like a lot of work? It is. And it's part of being a professional. It's part of having - and maintaining - high standards. Which is one thing that makes you a professional. And one thing that makes editors want to work with you again and again.

Zero tolerance for errors is quality control. Technical quality control.

Your query must also be perfect in another regard:

YOUR QUERY LETTER MUST BE WELL WRITTEN.

It has to be as good as you can possibly write it.

Now I'm referring to content, flow, continuity. It must be the best letter you can write. And if that means working on it for three weeks and rewriting it 15 times, then that's what it means.

Why? Because (and this is especially important if you have no writing credentials to put in the credibility paragraph)...

YOUR QUERY LETTER IS YOUR WRITING SAMPLE.

Am I a good writer?
Yes. Look at my letter. <u>This</u> is my writing.

So, to repeat what I hope is now unavoidably obvious, irrefutably necessary:

Your query letter must be perfect on <u>every</u> level (grammar, spelling, punctuation...content, structure, flow).

Do not send a letter with corrections made by hand.

Keeping working on the query for as long as it takes to get it right.

Am I nagging? Maybe. That's how important this is.
You'll thank me down the line.

LETTER # 2

134 E. 48 St.
New York, NY 10036
Mar. 18, 1991

Katherine Keller
Premiere Magazine
2 Park Avenue
New York, NY 10016

Ms. Keller:

I'm writing to suggest an article for the Cameos section of *Premiere*, profiling the sound engineer John Smith.

Mr. Smith was nominated for an Academy Award for *Dune* and is currently up for an Oscar for *Total Recall*. In addition, his contribution to the NBC mini-series, *Son of the Morning Star*, is under consideration for an Emmy.

Mr. Smith is highly respected in the film and television industries for his excellent work, which is grounded in the belief that with enough attention to the right details during shooting, dialogue and sound will not have to be replaced in postproduction. In a recent conversation, he told me that the producers of *Dune* expected to have to replace 75%-90% of the sound in the studio. Instead, they discovered they could actually use 75% of the sound as John had recorded it.

Often at the forefront of new developments in his field, Mr. Smith recorded the sound for *Tai-Pan*, which was the first major international production shot in China, and is about to start work on *Basic Instinct*, which will be the first major film to be recorded in 100% digital sound.

If you're interested in doing a Cameos profile on John Smith, I can be reached at the above address or at (212) 123-4567.

Sincerely,

Laura Gleason

LETTER #2

Paragraph 1:

Cameos is a section of the magazine that runs short pieces. Which means that Laura, by steering the editor to this section of the magazine, is cutting herself out of a feature article assignment. Why would she do this?

When I ask this question in a workshop, the usual answer is, "Because it's easier to break in to a magazine with a short article instead of a feature."

That's true. If you're a new writer, or you're trying to get published in a magazine for the first time (especially a high-end major publication), it <u>is</u> easier to break in with a shorter article, and this is an excellent strategy. An editor will be more likely to take a chance with a new writer on a short piece, targeted for a specialized section of the magazine, than with a feature.

But in this case there's another strategy at work. Laura is (as we'll see later) an experienced writer. She could pitch a feature, even though she's never written for *Premiere*. Yet she's not. Why?

Because she's pitching a story about a sound engineer, and she knows the magazine won't run a feature article on a sound engineer. In the film world, a sound engineer doesn't merit a feature. But Laura also knows that the magazine might run a smaller piece on a sound engineer. So that's what she's going for.

She doesn't want the editor to read her letter, assume she's pitching a feature on a sound engineer, and, on that basis alone, immediately reject her idea. So instead of risking that, she's steering the editor to the Cameos section. They won't do a <u>feature</u> on sound engineer, but they might do a Cameo.

If you have an idea that won't (or maybe won't) merit a feature, but might get published in a specialized section of the magazine you're pitching, steer the editor to that section. (And if that section of the magazine has its own editor, send your query to that editor.)

Paragraph 2:

Lots of information on John Smith. Why so much?

Because who the heck is John Smith? And why should this magazine want to do an article on him?... Well, <u>this</u> is who he is, and why he's worth an article.

In this letter, Laura is establishing the value of her <u>subject</u> (Smith), as opposed to <u>her</u> <u>knowledge</u> about the subject. (She's demonstrating her knowledge about Smith along the way, but the focus here is on Smith.)

Paragraph 3:

More information on Smith... Because who the heck is John Smith and why should this magazine want to do an article on him?

But now Laura is varying the information, adding specific details and accomplishments to the credentials (Smith's, not hers) she listed in the previous paragraph.

Laura is also doing something else: dropping a bit of film jargon to show she's familiar with the film industry, she can write about the film industry, and she can write about the film industry from an insider's perspective.

Be careful with jargon. When you use it, use enough to show that you know your subject and can write about it from the inside, but don't use so much that you lose the reader. You might also lose the editor. Even if you don't lose the editor, you might (and this could be worse) cause the editor to wonder if you'll use too much jargon when you write the article.

In paragraph 3 Laura is also indicating that she's spoken with Smith and she can deliver the interview.

Never pitch an interview without knowing you can get it. You don't have to <u>do</u> the interview before you get the assignment, but know you can <u>get</u> the interview. The easiest way to do this is to ask your subject if he's willing to be interviewed for the article. (And ask the question <u>before</u> you write the query.)

This doesn't apply when you're interviewing people <u>after</u> you've gotten the assignment. Those are two different situations. In the first, you're pitching the article. Which means you know you plan to interview someone. (Perhaps you plan to build the entire article around her.) In that case, speak to her to make sure she'll give you the interview, should you get the assignment. If you can't get the interview, you can't do the article.

In the second situation, you've gotten the assignment and you may not have known that you'd be interviewing a particular person. In this case, the person is a source (perhaps one among several), not the basis of the entire article. You couldn't let her know about the interview beforehand, because you may not have known you were going to interview her. And if you can't get the interview, you'll find someone else to talk to for the article.

Paragraph 4:

Still more about Smith.

Because Laura knows, going in, that this is going to be a hard sell. So she's giving the editor a lot of choices. If one topic doesn't grab the editor, there's another. If that doesn't interest the editor, there's yet another... Basically, Laura is saying, "Look at all the things we can write about this guy Smith."

Paragraph 5:

The close, with Laura's phone number.

But where's the credibility paragraph? Why has Laura left it out?

Because she's an established magazine writer, who's been published in more than a dozen magazines (including some extremely prestigious publications). When you get to that point, you can omit the credibility paragraph. But if you do, replace it with something. (Which Laura has done.)

As your career develops, and you get published in more and more magazines, you'll have too many credits to list them all in the credibility paragraph.

At any point in your career, you don't have to list more than six publications. More than six is overkill. Six is a good maximum because it shows you have experience, without being overwhelming or appearing that you're trying too hard.

As you accumulate more and more credits, you can (and should) choose the magazines you include in the credibility paragraph. At this point, fine-tune each query letter, picking the six titles that are most relevant.

What makes them relevant? The prestige of the publication. The fact that the article you wrote for that magazine is similar to the article (in content, tone, style, etc.) you're pitching. The fact that a magazine you were published in is similar (in content, tone, style, etc.) to the magazine you're pitching.

You can let an editor know you have more than six magazines to your credit by wording the paragraph something like: "My writing credits include _____, _____, _____, _____, _____, and _____, among other publications."

As your career progresses further, your resume will fill more and more space on the page. When your published credits (ideally, your magazine credits) fill the entire page (or almost fill the page), you can do what Laura does: Instead of the credibility paragraph, she simply slips her resume in with her query letter, and lets the resume speak for itself.

Laura got this assignment. But in this case, there's more to the story.

When the magazine responded to Laura's query, the editor said they wanted to do a story on John Smith, but they wanted the story to focus on his work for the film *Basic Instinct*.

So, Laura had written The Great Query Letter, and all the magazine wanted was one sliver of her idea.

Laura had to make a decision: She could have said, "No. I insist on doing this story <u>my</u> way. I want to write about what <u>I</u> want to write about."

Or, she could have listened to what the editor wanted, and agreed to write that.

Which is what she did. Laura's a professional.

And all that other good stuff about John Smith eventually went into two other articles Laura wrote for two other film magazines.

This is a situation you're very likely to find yourself in. Often.

My advice is: Everything being equal, you don't turn down an assignment.

No, this magazine isn't interested in all the information you've uncovered, or all the things you want to put in your article... But all that great stuff you know, that will make this article really work (at least the way <u>you</u> see the article), can go into another article (maybe several others) you write down the line for other magazines.

LETTER #3

1144 State St.
Chicago, IL 60612
July 11, 1984

Henry Pike
TV Guide
Radnor, PA 13571

Mr. Pike:

I'm writing to suggest an article for *TV Guide* on food stylists —
the highly skilled people who create the luscious-looking food we see
on TV commercials.

Actually, a good deal of the time what we're looking at isn't food at all,
but authentic-looking duplications that don't approach being edible.
When it is food, it's not in any condition to be eaten. A glistening turkey
might be coated with shellac. A piping hot, just-from-the-oven meal might
look that way due to burning rope giving off those wisps of "delectable
flavor fingers."

Tight-lipped and concerned with protecting trade secrets (and client
confidentiality), several food stylists have nevertheless agreed to be
interviewed for this piece, which I think would be ideal for your readers.
What I have in mind is not an exposé, but an entertaining, human
interest behind-the-camera look at an offbeat, unique field that affects
virtually everyone who watches television.

My magazine experience includes articles for *Entertainment Today*,
the *San Francisco Chronicle, Performing Arts Magazine, Ladies' Home
Journal, Hemispheres*, and *Modern Maturity*, among other publications.

I look forward to hearing for you. My phone number is (312) 123-4567.

Sincerely,

Tom Porter

LETTER #3

Notice this letter is different in tone and style? Why?

Because it's *TV Guide,* which has a unique voice. Not everyone can match that voice, and Tom is showing them that he not only knows their voice, but can write in their voice.

If you pitch a magazine that has a unique voice, show them you can write in their voice by writing your letter in that voice.

Paragraph 2:

Tom is demonstrating not only his knowledge of food stylists, but also an insider's knowledge of this field and the people in it. He's done his research, knows what he's talking about, and can put this knowledge in to words for the magazine's readers.

Paragraph 3:

Tom is telling the editor what he <u>won't</u> write: an exposé. Like Laura, in her query to *Premiere*, he's cutting himself out of a market by saying he won't write a certain type of article. Why?

When I ask this question in workshops, the answer I always get first is, "*TV Guide* doesn't publish exposés."

That's true, and it's a lesson in itself. If you know a magazine doesn't publish a certain type of article, don't pitch that kind of article to that magazine. You're only wasting your time and theirs.

Similarly, if an article can be structured several different ways (as most articles can be), think about the best way to pitch it to a particular magazine.

For example, an article on High Definition Television (HDTV) can be done as: 1) a new technology piece; 2) a service piece that reports on the high-definition televisions currently being made and tells consumers how to choose one; 3) a look at television (where it's been, where it's going); 4) an examination of the difficulties the government and the industry are having at arriving at a standard for HDTV; 5) an analysis of the importance of home entertainment in our culture. (Among other possibilities.)

If a magazine you want to pitch this article to doesn't publish new technology pieces (#1), general culture pieces (#3 and #5), or general news (#4), but does publish service pieces that help its readers understand and choose products (#2), pitch that article.

And make sure your query clearly communicates that's what you want to write. Don't make the editor have to read your mind (and take the risk that he might misread your mind), or interpret what you plan to do. Do that for him. Being clear makes everyone's job easier, ensures that the editor knows how you want to develop this idea, is better communication, and is just plain good writing.

So, Tom isn't going to pitch an exposé to *TV Guide*, because *TV Guide* doesn't publish exposés.

But even if *TV Guide* did publish exposés, Tom would have included this sentence in his letter. Why?

Because he was told, during his research, that the food stylists he'd be interviewing would not participate in an exposé. They had clients and industry standing to consider, and jobs and relationships to protect. Tom can't write an exposé, so he wants the editor to know that. The last thing he wants is *TV Guide* accepting the idea, and saying to him, "Let's rip the cover off the food-stylist industry!" He can't deliver that piece.

When you pitch an idea that has restrictions, let the editor know that in your query. You don't want an editor coming back to you and asking for something you can't give the magazine.

Paragraph #4:

The credibility paragraph is back in. Tom has been published in at least six magazines (perhaps more, but he doesn't need to go beyond six), and he's on his way to being able to include his resume instead of the credibility paragraph. But he's not there yet.

When he is there, he may decide not to do it. He may opt to always include the credibility paragraph. It's a matter of individual style and preference.

But never <u>not</u> establish your credibility. However you choose to do it, always let an editor know you've been published, and where you've been published.

LETTER #4

666 Sun Ct.
Los Angeles, CA 90035
Sept. 30, 1998

Bill Harrison
TV Guide
Radnor, PA 13571

Mr. Harrison:

Last week I watched, spellbound, as a killer entered a home,
stalked its occupants, and brutally murdered them one by one.

No, I was not present when these terrible events occurred, nor were the
murders real - they were a graphic re-creation of an actual crime I was
able to "witness" as a viewer of the TV show *Crime Gallery*.

But I felt as if I were present in that house, and the proliferation of such
shows has made us all vicarious witnesses to crimes of every type.
These programs can play a crucial role in the capture of criminals,
but how are they affecting us psychologically? Are Americans becoming
more aware of crime in our society, or desensitized to crime and
violence? Do criminologists and psychologists feel these shows are
beneficial or detrimental to our collective mental health?

I think an article that addresses these questions and issues is ideal
for *TV Guide*, and will be of great interest to your readers.

My magazine credits include articles for *North Coast View,
Better Health,* and *Manhattan Arts Magazine*.

I look forward to your reply, and can be contacted at (310) 123-4567.

Sincerely,

Ellen Dooley

LETTER #4

This letter is the exception I mentioned earlier.

The first three letters all had the same approach and tone: they were straightforward business letters. Even Letter #3, with its different style, took a business approach to the content.

Letter #4 represents another approach to the query letter: the "Grab 'em by the Throat" approach.

The idea is that you start your letter with something so funny, or cute, or provocative, or lurid, that you hook the reader and he just can't stop reading your letter. (In fact, a beginning like this is called a "hook".)

Generally, I don't use this approach. And I don't recommend it, because I believe it can backfire. What you think is cute, an editor might find silly or stupid. What you think is irresistibly intriguing, an editor might find offensive.

And this letter is a perfect example. When I use this letter in a workshop, the first thing I say after reading it out loud is, "Disregard the violence in the letter, and focus on the content."

For a while, I considered taking the letter out of the workshop packet. Then I realized it illustrates exactly why I don't recommend this approach: I'm trying to evoke interest in a magazine article by describing people getting murdered. Not very good taste.

So, my position on this type of letter is, rather than risk well-intentioned creativity backfiring, save your creativity for the article, and stick with the reliable businesslike query.

With some possible exceptions. This approach might work well with a humor magazine. And a good lurid letter could be perfect for a supermarket tabloid.

Now, I'm not saying that every query letter should be a straight business letter. Earlier, I said that when you pitch a magazine with a unique voice, use their voice in your letter. The same strategy can be applied to the opening of your query letter.

If you're pitching an idea for which mood, or setting, or description is important, you might begin your letter by setting the mood, evoking the setting, or writing a good description.

For example, if you were pitching an article about Romanian orphans, you might begin your letter with something like:

Five-month-old Natalia lies in her crib, barely moving. She is almost always silent, except when she cries in a pitifully weak voice that, if you were not in the room, you might not recognize as human. When she does cry, no one comes near to pick her up or offer so much as a quick comforting caress. Her empty eyes stare up at a bare ceiling, where water stains and peeling plaster are Natalia's only visual stimulation. What has Natalia done to merit such treatment? She was born into poverty, in a country where she and thousands like her are punished for simply being alive. Natalia is a Romanian orphan.

Hopefully you've described Natalia and her situation vividly enough to pique the editor's interest and make him want to keep reading. You're also demonstrating your knowledge of the topic, your writing style, and the style you'd probably use to do the article. (What you're not doing is being clever, cute, or lurid. All of which would be entirely inappropriate for this subject.)

Similarly, if you were pitching an article about a five-star resort, you might start your letter with a vivid, detailed, adjective-laden paragraph that evokes the luxury this resort offers its guests.

So, yes, there are times when you might be well served by writing a query letter that doesn't start as a straight business letter. And if you think this approach will strengthen your query - and bolster your chances of getting the assignment - by all means, try it.

But know what you're doing, and make your decisions consciously and carefully.

And after you get the editor's attention, be sure to include all the essential information every query should have.

All right... Now that we've written the perfect query letter, it's time to send it out.

SUBMISSIONS...

When it's time to send out the query, you come to a question all magazine writers face: Should I send out a multiple or an exclusive submission?

An **exclusive submission** is a query letter that's sent to one magazine. No other editors are sent that query until the first editor has rejected the idea.

A **multiple submission** is sent to several magazines at the same time. The editor who accepts it first is the one who gets to publish the article. (Or at least publish it first, which is very important in the magazine business.)

Editors prefer exclusive submissions, for the obvious reason: they're not competing with other editors for the same story. Some magazines take only exclusive submissions. They do not accept multiple submissions. The magazine's writer's guidelines, and *Writer's Market* profile, will tell you a magazine's submission policy.

It's a good idea to follow a magazine's submission policy. If you send a multiple submission to a magazine that does not accept multiple submissions, you're violating the magazine's submissions procedure and you'll probably get rejected.

This doesn't stop some writers from sending multiple submissions to magazines that don't accept them. Many of these writers simply don't mention it's a multiple submission. They often take the attitude, "It'll only be a situation I'll have to deal with if I get an acceptance." Or, "I'll worry about it when (and if) I have a problem." But if it does become a problem, it can be a <u>big</u> problem.

If you send a multiple submission to a magazine that does not accept multiple submissions, and you don't tell the editor it's a multiple submission, you could be dealing with something worse than rejection. Because if the editor calls to give you the assignment, and finds out (don't ask <u>how</u> she might find out - anything can happen, and many things do) you've sent the same query to another magazine, she could feel you've violated not only the magazine's submission policy, but her trust as well. (Especially when the magazine has clearly stated it accepts only exclusive submissions). Which certainly won't help your relationship with that editor or that magazine.

Also, if you send out multiple submissions, and don't say that's what you're doing, you run the risk that two editors will call and want the story. Then you're in an extremely awkward and relationship-damaging situation. You have to turn down one editor, which certainly won't help you build a relationship with that magazine (especially if the magazine has made it clear it doesn't accept multiple submissions). And there's no guarantee that the other editor (the one you don't turn down) won't find out what you've done, and who knows what <u>that</u> will do to your relationship with <u>him</u>. As a freelancer, you never want to damage relationships with people who are in a position to give you work.

Writers like multiple submissions because they cover more ground, and they do it faster. The standard response time to a query is six weeks. (More on this later.) So if you send out an exclusive submission, you may have to wait at least six weeks before you can move forward. And if you get a rejection and send out another exclusive query, you may have to wait another six weeks. Sometimes you don't hear from an editor within the six-week window and you have to send a follow-up letter. Getting an answer to <u>that</u> may also take six weeks.

If you want to send out multiple submissions, one way to do it safely is to pitch only magazines that accept multiple queries. But a lot of high-end magazines don't.

Does this mean we're completely at the mercy of magazines' submission policies? Not entirely.

There's a way around this dilemma. Which is the **parallel submission**. The parallel submission is simultaneous queries to magazines in different genres.

Remember your list of <u>types</u> of magazines? With the parallel submission, you pick one magazine from each category you've decided you're comfortable writing for, and pitch your article to these different types of magazines. Publications in different genres are not in competition with each other, so the editors generally don't mind if you're pitching the same idea to another type of magazine.

Going back to our initial idea: a small company in Santa Rosa is in a joint venture with GM to make electric cars... Our list of types of magazines included:

Automotive
Science/Technology
Regional
Environmental
Big Business/Entrepreneurial
Children's

You could send a query to one magazine in each genre. You'll have to fine-tune each query, shaping it to appeal to that editor, that magazine, and those readers, because each publication will be more (or less) interested in a particular aspect of the story.

If you get accepted by one magazine, and two days later you get a call from an editor at another publication, you don't have to (and you should not) hide the fact that you're already doing the piece for another magazine. The second editor is going to want a different story.

If you sell the same idea to two (or more) magazines...

YOU MUST WRITE
COMPLETELY DIFFERENT ARTICLES.

You can use the same sources...the same statistics...but you have to write a completely different piece (and use different quotations) for each magazine.

To some degree this will happen by itself, because each magazine is going to want a different slant, angle, emphasis, point of view.

Even so... Don't be lazy: Be prepared to - and make sure you do - write completely different articles for each magazine that accepts your idea.

But we've gotten ahead of ourselves.

Before you can get an acceptance, you have to send out the query letter. Which brings us back to what kind of submission you're going to choose: exclusive, multiple, or parallel.

So, you make that decision, and you send out your query (or queries).

What about sending queries by e-mail and fax?

I prefer to send the query by regular mail. E-mail can disappear into cyberspace at the touch of a button. Faxes can easily go lost between the fax machine and the editor's desk. I like to leave a paper trail. And having hard copies of my queries to sort, order, and file helps me keep track of things.

But that's me. You may not feel this way, and might be more (or very) comfortable sending your queries via e-mail or fax.

One more thing about e-mail going lost... I can't begin to count the number of times I've sent an e-mail or file to someone I was on a project with...who knew me, and who asked for the information... only to get a return e-mail or phone call saying the file went lost, or couldn't be opened, and would I please send it again. If you send an electronic communication to an editor who doesn't know you, doesn't know it's coming, and hasn't asked for it, and it goes lost, there is no way that editor is going to get in touch with you and ask you to send it again. The same goes for faxes. Something to think about.

However, you may approach a magazine that <u>wants</u> queries sent electronically. High-tech magazines generally do. Web magazines always do.

So, when it comes to regular mail vs. electronic communication... If you have a preference (and the choice is yours), do what you prefer to do. If a magazine indicates it wants a query sent a particular way, that's what you should do.

If you send queries by regular mail...

ALWAYS INCLUDE AN SASE
(SELF-ADDRESSED STAMPED ENVELOPE).

You don't have to mention it in your letter. Just put a stamp and your name and address on a standard #10 (long white) envelope, fold it in thirds, and slip it in with the query. They'll find it.

This, too, is non-negotiable. Magazines receive dozens, hundreds, perhaps thousands, of queries a month. They are not going to pick up the tab for postage. Most magazines will not respond to a query letter that does not include an SASE.

Sound like more rules? More Do's and Don'ts? It is. It's also another aspect of being professional. After a while, you won't even think about these things. You'll do them automatically. That, too, is part of being professional.

If being professional isn't enough motivation for you, consider this: You're competing against all the other freelancers out there. You want to write for a certain magazine? Well, so do a lot of them. And every time you send out a query, you're being compared, consciously or not, to all of them.

If I'm an editor reading your query, and you're doing things wrong, or not doing things right, or not doing things you should be doing, or making my life harder and my day busier... Why would I choose to work with you, when I have a stack of letters on my desk from other writers who are doing things right? They're not raising any of the red flags you are. They're not giving me any of the problems I suspect or fear you will. Why take the time to bring you along, and show you how to do it correctly, when I've got all these others who are already doing it right?

Set high standards for yourself...stick to your standards...be professional...and you won't be in this situation. You'll get more respect from the people you work with... And your writing will be better.

Am I nagging again?

Well, an amazing number of new writers don't pay attention to the basics.

But you will.

So, let's get back to the query letter you've sent out.

When I send out a query letter, is there a risk that my idea will be stolen?

Yes, there is that risk. Does it happen? Not really.

You can't copyright an idea. By law, it can't be done. So, yes, any time you put an idea out there, there's the possibility it could be stolen. But that rarely actually happens. It just isn't in a magazine editor's best interest to do it.

Editors need us. They depend on us for new ideas. If you've come up with an idea an editor likes well enough to want to steal, that editor has much more to gain by establishing a relationship with you. You've come up with one good idea...who knows how many others you'll come up with? If you're that good, why wouldn't the editor want an ongoing relationship with you? So they have more to gain by not stealing ideas.

Not that it never happens. But when a magazine gets a reputation for stealing ideas, the word gets out and writers stop sending ideas. So in this way, too, editors have much more to gain by being straight with us.

(But...the mere possibility that an idea can be stolen is a reason for not revealing <u>everything</u> in your query letter. If something is stolen, the more you reveal, the more you lose. When you write a query, you should strike a balance: Include whatever you need to, to pique the editor's interest, without "giving away the store.")

Much more common than outright theft is that when you send your query, the magazine has already assigned a story very much like yours, or someone else has sent in the same idea and the editor chooses that writer. Then the magazine rejects you, and four months later there's your story. They haven't stolen it. It's just that if you're thinking about something, there's a good chance other people out there (and all it takes is one) are thinking about the same thing.

All right... The query is out. Now you wait for an answer.

And one of three things happens:
You get ignored.
You get rejected.
You get an assignment.

Let's start with getting ignored.

The standard window for a response to a query is six weeks. Sometimes you get a response after only a few days. (Fast answers are almost always rejections.) Sometimes you get a response after only a few weeks. (Actually, most answers are rejections.) Sometimes you don't get any response at all.

If you don't get an answer in six weeks, it's time to send a follow-up letter. Which brings us to Letter #5. (Remember: ALL correspondence with magazines should include an SASE.)

LETTER #5

1234 Main St.
San Francisco, CA 94123
July 1, 1980

Donna Riston
Redbook
2468 Park Ave.
New York, NY 10036

Ms. Riston:

In May I sent you a query letter proposing an article for *Redbook* on framing and display.

As of this date, I haven't yet heard from you.

I realize that evaluating all the queries you receive takes time, and my initial letter might still be under consideration.

But it's also possible that you never received my first letter, and on that chance I'm enclosing a copy for your convenience.

I'm still interested in doing this article for *Redbook*, and can be reached at the above address or at (415) 123-4567.

Sincerely,

Mike Brautler

LETTER #5

What does Letter #5 does <u>not</u> have?

Attitude.

It is not accusatory or blaming. No anger. It's a polite business letter in which Mike is simply reminding the editor that he sent her a query, and letting her know he hasn't gotten an answer.

Mike may be frustrated, or angry, or insulted, but that is not going to find its way into his letter. This letter is not about expressing his feelings. It's about moving the process along, so he'll know what to do next with this idea.

Mike is also enclosing a copy of his first letter (he just prints out the first letter and slips it in, unsigned, with this one), in case the editor decides she likes his idea but can't find the first letter. Where is it?... In her hand.

Letter #5 is your basic follow-up letter, sent when you don't get an answer to your query.

And sometimes you still don't get an answer.

So you wait another four weeks, and then send Letter #6. (Now we're shortening the window from six weeks to four. They've already had six weeks. They can have more time, but you need to know if they're interested in this idea, because if they're not, you want to send it to another magazine.)

LETTER # 6

1234 Main St.
San Francisco, CA 94123
Aug. 1, 1980

Donna Riston
Redbook
2468 Park Ave.
New York, NY 10036

Ms. Riston:

In May I sent you a query letter proposing an article for *Redbook* on framing and display.

I did not get a response, and at the beginning of July I sent you a second letter and a copy of my article proposal.

As of this date, my second letter has also gone unanswered, so I'm writing again to suggest an article about framing and display. I'm also including my initial query, to save you the time of looking for it.

I am still very interested in doing this article for *Redbook*. I also appreciate how busy you are, so if I do not hear from you by September 5th I will assume you feel this idea is not right for *Redbook* and I will feel free to submit it elsewhere.

I can be reached at the above address or at (415) 123-4567.

Sincerely,

Mike Brautler

LETTER #6

Again...No Attitude. No accusations. No anger.

By now, Mike may be very frustrated, or very angry, or very insulted. But that is not going to find its way into this letter. Like Letter #5, this communication isn't about expressing his feelings. It's about moving the process along so Mike will know what to do next.

At this point you just want a response, even if it's a rejection. Because a rejection is better than no response at all. If this is an exclusive submission, you can't move forward with the idea until you hear from this editor. Even if it's a multiple submission, and you can send it elsewhere, you still want a response.

Because, first of all, you're entitled to one.

And second, an idea isn't dead at a particular magazine until you hear from the editor that it's dead. There have been times when I didn't hear from an editor until I sent Letter #6, and then it turned out that the magazine <u>was</u> interested in the idea. I have no idea why the editor didn't respond sooner. He just didn't. And it didn't matter - he wanted to give me the assignment. So until you hear that they don't want the idea, there's always the chance that they do.

Letter #6 recaps the situation, mentions Letter #5, and again Mike includes a copy of his initial query.

But what has Mike done in paragraph four? He's politely added a deadline. Not an ultimatum (as someone in one workshop called it). A deadline. Mike has politely let the editor know that if he doesn't receive a response by a clearly-stated time (about four weeks), he will feel free to submit this idea elsewhere.

This covers him, in case he sends the query to another magazine, that editor wants it, and _then_ Mike hears from the first editor, who has decided he wants it, too .

What happens if I don't get a response to Letter #6?

If you don't get a response to Letter #6, the magazine probably isn't interested in your idea. What you do then, is up to you.

You could give up on that magazine, and concentrate on other magazines that might want the idea.

I keep sending follow-up letters. Until I finally do hear from the magazine. The very fact that I'm not hearing from the editor indicates there's no interest in this idea, but I don't know what's going on at the magazine. There may be other reasons why I'm not getting a response. So I keep at it until I get that rejection letter.

Unless I get an acceptance from another magazine. At that point, my focus isn't getting an answer from a magazine editor I have to chase down. My focus is doing the best job I can for the editor that's given me an assignment.

A variation on this scenario is, after trying unsuccessfully to sell one idea, I get another, and put my energy in to pitching that one. When that happens, it's easy for an old idea, which you haven't been able to sell, to fall through the cracks while you focus on your new idea.

And some writers never give up on an idea.

It's up to you: How you work, how much energy you have, how focused you are, and how long you can (and do) stay with one thing before you move on to something else.

About those cracks, and things falling through them...

Part of being disciplined is <u>not</u> having things fall through the cracks. There are times when I <u>allow</u> things to fall through the cracks, because there's something else I want to put my time and energy in to... But if you're disciplined, and focused (which you should be), something shouldn't simply "fall through the cracks" unless you choose to let it.

That covers what happens when you <u>don't</u> hear from a magazine.

Now let's talk about what happens when you <u>do</u>.

That's going to be either an acceptance or a rejection.

Let's talk about rejection.

Rejections come faster than acceptances. One editor, acting alone, can reject an article proposal. Acceptances take longer because there's more involved in accepting an idea. At bigger magazines, they're often discussed at editorial meetings.

Rejections come in the mail. So if you send out a query, and a week later you go to your mailbox and there's an envelope with a magazine logo as the return address... Don't get excited. It's going to be a rejection.

Rejections come in all shapes and sizes. The most common is the form letter. Which is notoriously impersonal.

Some magazines have a large rubber stamp, imprinted with all the reasons your idea might be rejected. Next to each reason is a box. They slap the stamp on a sheet of paper (or a post card), then check off the box next to the reason they're rejecting you.

I've gotten my own query letter back as a rejection. Once, my rejection came in the form of my query letter, on the bottom of which an editor had scrawled "NO!"

Most of the time you don't know why you're being rejected. The standard reason is: Does not meet our editorial needs. Which says it all, really.

The idea might be wrong for that magazine. The idea might have been right for the magazine at another time, say two months ago, but isn't right any more. The magazine might have already covered the topic. Or it might have covered one aspect of the topic. Or it might have covered a similar topic. Or the editor might <u>think</u> the magazine has covered the topic, whether it has or not, or whether it covered the topic the way <u>you</u> want to cover it. But all these reasons, and all the variations on them, come back to the same thing: the article does not meet the magazine's editorial needs.

Sometimes rejections are a little less impersonal. You might get a rejection letter on the bottom of which (or in the margin of which) an editor has scribbled something like: "Not this time. Try us again." Or: "Sorry, but keep trying." Or any variation on this.

Congratulations. You've just made contact with an editor who cares enough to take an extra five seconds to make what can be a brutally streamlined process a little more human.

If you query the same magazine with another idea, send your query to this editor. (Unless you're targeting a special section of the magazine, that has its own editor.) This second letter (and future queries to this editor) can be a little more personal. Remind the editor that you've queried her in the past and, though she rejected your previous idea, she invited you to try again. Well, now you're trying again.

And keep sending your queries to this editor (as long as they're appropriate for her magazine). Sometimes a relationship is built this way. It's a relationship built on rejection, but I know people who wound up getting assignments from such relationships.

A few words about rejection...

It's going to happen. It's going to happen a lot. In fact, you're going to get rejected more than you're going to get accepted. It's the nature of the beast.

My best advice on handling rejection: Don't take it personally.

It simply means your idea isn't right for that magazine at that time. (Or maybe your idea is right for the magazine, but the editor doesn't think so or can't see it.) All rejection means is, you're not going to get that story published in that magazine.

Getting rejected does not mean your idea is bad, you're a bad writer, you're a failure, or you're a bad person.

It can mean you wrote a bad query letter.

So when you get rejected, you should look at your query to see if there's anything wrong, or any way you can make it better.

Then, move on. Send the query to the next magazine on your list.

But...

ALWAYS FINE-TUNE YOUR QUERY.

Don't just cut and paste the letter into a new document and send it out again. Rework the letter as much as necessary so it speaks directly to the editor at this magazine... So that it takes this magazine, and its needs, and its readers, and its voice, and its submission policies into account, and is truly the best letter you can possibly send to the magazine you're pitching now.

Nobody likes being rejected. But remember that you're competing against all the other freelance writers out there, plus editors who are also thinking of ideas. Add to that...once a magazine covers a story, it isn't very likely to print another story on the same topic, or on a closely-related topic, for some time. Add to <u>that</u>...there's only so much space in any magazine for all the stories its editor may want to publish... And you begin to get some perspective on why so many story ideas are rejected.

BUT...story ideas are also accepted. And magazines have an ongoing need for new ideas. So, just as getting rejected is often a matter of numbers, so is the possibility of getting an acceptance.

And if you keep trying... If you keep sending out queries, and if you're doing it right... If you have ability as a writer, your ideas are good, and your timing is good... The chances are in your favor that sooner or later you're going to get that acceptance.

And now, finally, let's talk about <u>that</u>.

GETTING AN ACCEPTANCE...

Acceptances usually come by phone. I once received a letter from an editor, saying the magazine wanted my idea and asking me to call her so we could discuss the assignment. That was unusual. Most often, when an editor wants to give you an assignment she'll pick up the phone and call, because there's a lot to discuss.

During this conversation, she'll volunteer most of the essential information. If she doesn't volunteer information, it's OK to ask. There are specific things you need to know when getting a writing assignment.

And this is what you need to discuss:

How long will the article be?
When does the editor want the finished article?
How much will you get paid?
How will you get paid?
Does the magazine pay expenses?
Does the magazine have a kill fee?
What rights is the magazine buying?

You'll also discuss any other questions and issues relevant to the assignment. Like, does the editor want you to write the article exactly as you described it in your proposal, or does she want you to focus on a particular element or aspect of the story? Does she want a certain slant or angle on the story? Is there something in your proposal that she doesn't want in the article, or doesn't want given as much prominence as you gave it in your proposal?

How long will the article be?

This is your **word count** - the number of words the editor wants you to write.

The formatting standard is 250 words/page (double spaced). So if you're asked for a 2,000-word article, the editor wants eight pages. If she asks for 10 pages, she wants 2500 words.

When calculating the length of your article, think words, not manuscript pages or number of lines on a page. The number of pages in a manuscript (and the number of lines on a page) can vary, depending on your computer, your page setup, your font, and your point size. The best (and by far the easiest) way to track the length of your piece is to use your computer's word count.

(And the number of words (not pages or lines per page) is what really matters. Before your article is published, it goes into layout, and font and point size will very probably change.)

When does the editor want the finished article?

This is your deadline.

Generally, magazine deadlines are reasonable, typically two-four months. (Or more.) They want you to do a good job. They don't want you racing the clock or the calendar.

How much will you get paid?

Money is secondary. The important thing is to get published. But, here's a general idea of magazines pay scales:

High end:	$750 and up	($1/word)
Mid-range:	$300 - $ 700	($.50 - $.75/word)
Low end:	$250 and down	(to as low as $0/word)

Keep in mind that whether you're getting paid "a lot" or "a little" is extremely relative, with lots of variables.

One of the biggest variables is, have you been published before? If you've never been published, the first time you break in to print (even if you're paid "only" $100, or, for that matter, $25) you're being paid a lot. You're going from unpublished to published, and that's worth plenty!

Similarly, while you're building your resume it's worth it to you to get published anywhere you can. So, again, regardless of the dollar-amount you're paid, you're getting something valuable in return for your writing.

Even when you're established, there are times when it's worth it to you to work for a lower-paying magazine because you might be breaking into a new area, or adding the name of a particular magazine to your resume. There, too, you're being compensated with more than whatever figure happens to follow the dollar sign on your invoice.

Another extremely important variable is your word count. According to the above chart, $250 is a low-end amount. But how much are you being asked to write? One thousand words, or 250 words? If you're getting $250 to write 250 words, you're certainly not working on the low end of the pay scale! Flipping the coin (so to speak), if you're getting $500 to write 3,000 words, you're working for about $.16 a word. Quite a bit below the mid-range arena the chart suggests.

So, before you decide whether you're getting paid a lot or a little, take all the variables into account.

Then consider this: Until you're making your (entire) living as a writer, it doesn't matter. Money isn't the only way you're compensated. And as long as you're getting <u>something</u> out of it (prestige, a longer resume, experience, contacts, personal satisfaction, self-esteem), it's worth it.

Even when you are making your living (entirely) as a writer, there are times when it's worth it to work for less than you want to or less than you normally would. Because you're getting something in return, other than money.

How will you get paid?
There are three ways to get paid:
On Acceptance
On Publication
On Speculation

On Acceptance: You write the piece, the editor looks it over, accepts it for publication, and you get paid. (You're approved to get paid. The check may not go out for another 30 days.)

It doesn't matter when the magazine publishes the article. Once the editor agrees to publish it...once the magazine accepts it for publication...you get paid.

High-end magazines usually pay on acceptance.

On Publication: You write the piece, the magazine decides to publish it, you get paid when it gets published.

Which might be months down the line. So you get paid months down the line. And if the article is scheduled for publication in August, and there's a change in the magazine's production schedule and it gets bumped back to September, or October, they don't have to pay you until September or October. That's the deal. (They might pay you in August, but they don't have to.)

Mid-range and low-end magazines often pay on publication.

On Speculation: You write the piece. They look it over. If they decide not to publish it - for any reason whatsoever - you do not get paid.

You still own the piece, and you can try to sell it elsewhere, but of course there's no guarantee you will sell it elsewhere.

Magazines across the spectrum pay on speculation. A low-end magazine might pay on spec because it doesn't have money to risk on articles it may not publish. Or it may not have the money to take a chance on a new writer (or a writer who hasn't written for that magazine before). Or because it doesn't have the budget for an editor to give an assignment because he thinks he <u>might</u> want to cover that topic.

Some high-end magazines pay on spec when they work with new writers. It's a form of insurance: "Yes, we'll take a chance on you. But because you're a new writer, we want insurance. If it doesn't work out, we don't want to have to pay for taking this chance."

Some magazines pay on spec the first time they work with any writer. Some very prestigious publications pay on spec as a matter of policy. One reason they might do this is they're constantly approached by writers they've never worked with, and it makes it less risky to work with writers they don't know.

No professional writer likes to work on spec. And there are times when we all do. Would you turn down a top national magazine or newspaper because it pays on spec, or because the editor wants to pay you on spec your first time out with that publication?

Does the magazine pay expenses?
Some magazines (usually high-end publications) pay the expenses of a writer on assignment.

Standard expenses are:

Phone   (Calls to interview people or get information.)

Gas   (If you have to drive somewhere for the article.)

Parking (If you have to drive somewhere for the article.)

Tolls   (If you have to drive somewhere for the article.)

Some magazines will pick up other expenses, like the price of admission to a show or exhibition you might have to attend to do the piece. Or a meal in a restaurant if you're interviewing someone for the magazine. (Not an interview you decide to do as part of your research, after you've gotten the assignment. An interview you have to do (and told them you'd be doing, in your query) because that person is the focus of your article.)

When you discuss expenses, nail down exactly which expenses the magazine will pay. Each magazine has its own policy regarding expenses. Some are very tight, some are very generous.

Editors don't always volunteer that the magazine pays expenses. If an editor doesn't volunteer this information, and if you'll incur expenses while doing a story (you'll know, because that's part of your research for the piece before you pitch it), ask if the magazine pays expenses.

Once I was getting an assignment from a major national magazine. When the editor didn't volunteer that they'd pay my expenses, I asked. Her response was, "What expenses do you anticipate?"

She wasn't challenging me or testing me. She was just asking a question. It's a question you should be prepared to be asked, and be prepared to answer. (You know, because you've done your homework.)

I told her, "I plan to do a lot of telephone interviewing."

She immediately responded, "Oh, of course we'll pay your phone expenses!"

It was such a given that she simply forgot to mention it.

So far, I've been talking about expenses you'll incur when you're doing an article from home. If a magazine sends you somewhere on assignment (the editor contacts you and asks you to write an article you didn't propose), it will pay your expenses. If it has the money to do it, and if that's their policy. Which it should be (they're contacting you and asking you to go somewhere for them), and is - at high-end publications. (An editor at a big-name magazine isn't going to call you and say, "We'd like you to go half-way across the country to do a story for us. And while you're there, find a cheap hotel because we're not paying your expenses for this.")

Some mid-range and low-end magazines send writers on assignments that require some travel, but don't pay expenses. For example, a low-end magazine might ask you to do a story that requires you to spend the night (or weekend) in a nearby town, but you have to pay for your own food and lodging. If you take the assignment, after you cover your expenses you might not make any money. If your writing fee doesn't cover your expenses, it can even cost you money.

This situation, and variations on it, aren't uncommon. What do you do?

Well, what do you <u>want</u> to do? You can always turn down any assignment you're offered. But it might be worth it to you to take the assignment if it means you'll get published. It's a judgment call.

It's hard for a new writer, who has a chance to get published, to turn down an assignment. (Some writers with years of experience and very respectable resumes never turn down assignments.) In the end, you have to live with whatever decision you make. Sometimes it's worth it to not make money on an assignment...or perhaps lose money...because you're getting something (whatever it may be) in return. Sometimes it isn't worth it. (We're back to those variables.)

While we're on this subject...

Because many publishers and editors (in all writing markets) know how important it is for new writers to get published, sometimes the only thing you're offered is "exposure".

This is something you'll often see in ads seeking writers. Sometimes you get paid in copies of the magazine (common with small fiction publications). Sometimes <u>all</u> you get is exposure. If it's worth it to you, for any reason, to take an assignment or job, to do the work...then do it. If you decide it isn't worth it, don't do it. Either way you might make a smart decision. Either way you may come to regret it later.

Sooner or later we all make a decision we come to feel bad about. (Most of us can reel off several decisions we regret to varying degrees.) The important thing is to learn from each decision you make, and so become a better person, and a better writer, and a better practitioner of the business of writing.

Does the magazine have a kill fee?

You write a perfectly publishable piece. The magazine decides not to publish it for some reason that has nothing to do with the quality of your writing. (Maybe the magazine's editorial policy has changed. Maybe the topic is no longer relevant or timely.) Your piece does not get published, but you get paid for your time and effort. That's a **kill fee**.

Kill fees are sometimes flat rates (say, a $250 kill fee), or they can be a percentage of your fee for doing the article (say, 25% - you were going to get $600 for the article, the kill fee kicks in, you get $150.)

When you're paid a kill fee, the magazine does not publish the article; you get the money; you still own the piece; you're free to try to sell it elsewhere.

Not all magazines have kill fees. If you're working for a magazine that doesn't have a kill fee, and your piece is not suitable for publication (or they don't accept it), you simply don't get paid. (You still own the piece, and you're free to try to sell it elsewhere.)

Depending on the magazine, there might be a kill fee if they don't publish your article for a reason that <u>does</u> have to do with the quality of your writing (the piece isn't written well or doesn't meet the needs of the magazine). However, with most publications, if you turn in a manuscript they can't use because you have not written a good article, you haven't fulfilled your obligation to the magazine and they will reject the piece and not pay you.

Many editors don't volunteer that their magazine has a kill fee. If they don't volunteer it, you can ask. But many times I don't. I assume I'm going to write a piece that they will publish, and so the kill fee isn't an issue. That's not to say I never ask. But most of the time I just let it go.

Another reason I don't ask is, it has the potential to raise a red flag. Kind of like, "Oh? Do you expect something to go wrong?"

But that's me. I've just never put that much energy in to kill fees. Are you going to turn down an assignment because a magazine <u>doesn't</u> pay a kill fee?

There are times I do ask. Part of doing your homework, and part of being professional, is understanding the deal you're making with a magazine...understanding the terms of your agreement, from both ends. And that includes knowing if there's a kill fee. Besides, you're entitled to know.

What happens if the magazine says it doesn't accept my article, and then publishes it?

Feeling a little paranoid?

This rarely happens. (I'd like to say it never happens, but anything <u>can</u> happen.) It hardly ever happens because, like stealing your idea when you submit a query, magazines have more to gain by <u>not</u> ripping off writers. If you've written an article an editor likes well enough to want to steal, he has much more to gain by treating you well, and having you write more articles for him.

That's not to say that bad things don't happen out there. If an editor, or a magazine, or a publisher, deals with you dishonestly or treats you unfairly, you have recourse. You can lodge a complaint (which might have legal ramifications), and you can put the word out among writers, giving the offender a bad reputation and making it harder for them to find other writers to work with. (You'll find information on how to do this in the Resources section.) The situation may or may not be resolved the way you'd like it to be, but at least you've felt you've done <u>something</u>.

And, just as you can turn to these resources if you've been treated unfairly or dealt with dishonestly, you should consult these resources <u>before</u> you work with anyone you have a question or doubt about.

What rights is the magazine buying?

When a magazine publishes an article, it purchases specific rights to that material. (No, you don't get paid separately - this is part of what your fee covers.) You should always know what rights are being bought.

On page 139 is a list of rights and what they mean. (This is a very general list. It does not include every kind of rights, and the explanations are basic. You can find a fuller discussion of rights in *Writer's Market* and books dealing with copyright law and contracts.)

Generally, high-end magazines buy all rights. That's one reason they're paying the big bucks. Generally, magazines that pay less, buy fewer rights. (They pay less, they get less.)

Unlike the kill fee, which I often don't bring up, rights are something I always ask about. Even so, I've never put that much energy into what rights a magazine is buying. (Certainly not as much energy as some writers I know.)

One reason is, I've worked for a lot of high-end magazines, and they generally buy all rights.

When I've pitched mid-range or low-end magazines, rights were more of an issue, but in those situations I was concerned with other things. There was a reason I'd gone after that publication. I might have been breaking into a new subject area, and a mid-range or low-end magazine might have been the only publication I could sell on the idea. I knew I'd be getting less money (and the magazine would be buying fewer rights) going in. And anyway, my focus wasn't on either money or rights. It was on breaking in to a new subject area, or adding a certain type of magazine to my resume. With that to gain, I wasn't going to get hung up on rights. But that's me.

I've always believed that, for new writers, it's more important to get published than to worry about rights. Not everyone would agree. And that's another example of my not putting as much energy into rights as other people. I've found that rights take care of themselves.

I'm not saying that rights don't matter, or that I don't care about rights. You should always know what rights you're selling when anyone purchases your work. This is important, and it can be extremely important.

For example, you plan to write a book. While you're working on the book, you're able to sell a magazine article on the same topic. You want to include this article (or substantial parts of it) in your book, but the magazine buys all rights. What do you do?

You work this out with the editor when you get the assignment. Most editors will have no problem with your including this material in your book. Why should they? It makes their magazine look good. They may ask for a credit that states the material first appeared in say, *Global Quest* (which is what makes their magazine look good), and they're entitled to that.

But in order to work out such details with an editor, you have to make him aware of the situation (you want to include this material in a book), you have to come to an agreement with each other, and you have to know what rights the magazine is buying.

Another reason rights are important is, you don't always know what you'll want to do with this material down the line. Or what situations might come up after the article is published. (Another publication could want to publish this article. Someone might want to include .it in their newsletter. A Web site might want to post it.) Knowing what rights you've sold makes you better equipped to deal with future situations and make informed decisions.

There's also the psychological component to consider. You should know what rights you're selling because it's your work. And it's part of being professional.

Imagine this conversation...

"I just got an assignment from a magazine!"

"Congratulations. What rights are they buying?"

"I have no idea."

What's your gut-level response to this writer?

Mine is, "New kid on the block. Has a lot to learn."

Let's take the conversation a few exchanges further...

"Didn't they tell you?"

"No."

"Didn't you ask?"

"No."

"Why not?"

"I don't know." / "It didn't occur to me." / "I have no idea."

What's your gut-level response now?

Mine is, "Doesn't take himself seriously as a writer."

I may not put a lot of energy into rights, but I always make sure I know what rights I'm selling, and I always <u>think</u> about what rights I'm selling. And I've been in situations (not with magazines) where I'm made rights a negotiation issue, and a deal-breaking issue at that. I take myself - and my writing - very seriously.

One reason some writers do put a lot of energy into rights is secondary rights. **Secondary rights** give you the chance to sell the same piece (the exact same piece, not just the idea) to more than one publication. Which means you're earning money from work you've already done. There are many writers who pursue the secondary rights market avidly. I've never been one of them.

Which isn't to say that I don't care about secondary rights, or that I've <u>never</u> gone after this market. But as I've built my career, and gotten more work...more assignments...more projects...I usually found myself going on to new things rather than staying with things I'd already written, pieces that were already published. So, rather than actively pursue the secondary rights market, I kept moving on.

Judgment call. Was I right? Was I being lax or lazy? Some people might say I was. But I've never regretted it. We make our decisions and we live with them. Another writer might say I've made a big mistake by not going after this potentially lucrative market.

If the secondary rights market appeals to you, go for it. You might be one of those writers who <u>really</u> pursues it. Or you might decide that you have other things to do.

It's your career. It's your life. Do what works for you.

We left you on the phone with that editor who called to give you an assignment. Let's finish that conversation.

After you discuss the essentials, you'll discuss any situational variables, which will include any special requests or preferences the editor may have regarding this story.

While you're having this conversation, take notes. This is an amazingly informal process, and most of the time there is no written contract.

Your notes will help you remember what's been agreed to, help you keep track of things like your word count and deadline, and remind you what to expect with this assignment.

The fact that there's usually no contract surprises many new writers. For people used to a more formal way of doing business, it can be unsettling. But it's not something you should spend a lot of time worrying about.

Magazine editors rarely go back on what they've agreed to. There's no reason for them to. What they're offering is standard magazine policy. They don't have anything to gain by going back on the agreement.

If you're uncomfortable with such informality, you can ask for a contract or a letter of agreement. If an editor hasn't already mentioned a contract, she probably won't want to take the time to prepare either one. In which case, you can offer to draft an informal letter with the details of the conversation, and ask her to sign off on it and send it back to you. All you're asking her to do is initial a letter. No reason for her to say no to that.

I've always done it however the editor wanted to do it. And with all the articles I've written, only once did something "go wrong" (I wasn't paid the amount I was promised), and after a little dogged pursuit on my part (which, admittedly, took a few strange twists and turns), everything was straightened out.

I'm not saying you'll never encounter problems. Every writer has his or her share of war stories, and writers' Web sites have (growing) lists of magazines, publishers, individuals, and companies with whom writers have had problems. When you look at these lists, you see a preponderance of three types of people and places: start-ups, low-end publications, and people who target new writers.

Starts-ups can (and certainly do) go out of business. Sometimes after only a few months or only an issue or two. If it's a low-end start-up, it probably pays on publication. If you have a piece scheduled for publication a few months down the line, and the magazine doesn't last that long, you might not get paid. Or you might be paid pennies on the dollar (which weren't all that much to begin with). That's one of the potential problems with working with a new magazine.

Low-end magazines sometimes have cash-flow problems. And if those problems get worse, sometimes suppliers (of all sorts, but certainly including writers) don't get paid. That's one of the potential problems with working with low-end magazines.

And there are people who target - and sometimes prey on - new writers. With the advent and growth of the Internet, they have more opportunity than ever, and are certainly taking advantage of it.

There are Web sites that offer writers the chance to get published, in return for which they receive exposure (but no money). That's not automatically bad (and it's not preying on writers), because for a new writer exposure is everything and money is secondary. (And even if the site goes under, you can still legitimately claim it as a writing credit.) But some sites charge writers a fee for submitting their work (or getting published). That is preying on writers. One thing you do not want to do is pay someone to publish your writing. (Not a magazine article. People pay subsidy publishers to publish books they can't sell elsewhere all the time. That's different. However, you should not pay someone to publish something like a magazine article.)

There are situations where you do pay to have your writing looked at. Like paying a reading or evaluation fee to a literary agent who might represent you if he feels your work is salable. And paying a fee to enter your work in a contest.

I am not in favor of contest fees. But I am in favor of entering contests. Sometimes you can't do one without doing the other. If you want to enter a contest that charges a fee...if you feel you have enough to gain, even though you'll be paying that fee...do it. I have.

As for literary agents who charge a fee to read your work... Again, if you feel there's enough to gain, do it. But be aware of this: Literary agents do not handle magazine writers.

It isn't worth it to them. If an agent has a client who's a book writer, and the client is approached by a magazine to do an article, the agent might handle that as a courtesy or service to the client. But literary agents do not accept as clients writers who exclusively do magazine work. And magazine writers do not need agents. They can get assignments on their own.

Ultimately, there's no guarantee you won't get burned somewhere along the way. Always try to use good judgment and think something through carefully before you do it. If something bad does happen, learn from it, move on, and try not to repeat the same mistake. And there'll be times when you won't have made a mistake. You simply encountered someone who was going to cheat or do something bad to whomever they happened to cross paths with, and you happened to be one of those people.

But this discussion started on a happier note - you'd just gotten an assignment.

Congratulations!

Now, let's talk about writing the article.

WRITING THE ARTICLE...

Remember college? And how, when you had a paper to write, or a book to read, or a test to study for, you'd often put it off to the last minute, and then pull an all-nighter and (try to) whip it off? Well, this isn't that.

<u>Don't wait for the last minute to write the article</u>. The deadline will almost always be reasonable, but a thousand things can go wrong, and a thousand-and-one often do. Don't put yourself under the extra pressure and stress of not only having to write the article, but having to race a deadline. It won't be fun, and it will show in the writing.

Obviously, a lot more can be said about writing a magazine article. But that's another book. Given the amount of space I have here, my best advice is:

Don't wait for the last minute.

Manage your time well.

Don't be lazy. Do whatever you have to, to make the article as good as it can be.

Keep working on the piece (rewriting, revising, editing) until it's as good as it can be.

When you think it's done, put it away for a day or two. Then go back to it with a fresh eye and see if there's anything else you can do to make it better.

Then read it out loud to someone. If necessary, work on it some more.

Why should you read it out loud to someone?

Because reading it out loud is one of the best ways to edit and proofread your writing. The ear and the brain work differently from the eye and the brain. At this point, you've read your work a hundred times and you're probably missing things. Reading it out loud, you'll pick up things that are getting by you. And if you're reading it to someone, they'll hear things you're still missing. I am always amazed that, with all the years I've been doing this, and after all the times I've read something on the computer screen, I will still find things to correct or change the first time I read it out loud. Even when I'm sure it's perfect.

If you don't have someone handy to read your work to, read it to yourself. Out loud. You might feel a little silly, but it's worth it. If it helps, stand in front of a mirror when you read. Still feel silly? It's still worth it.

Remember...Like the query letter, the article has to be as good as it can possibly be.

The standard manuscript format is 25 lines to a page, double spaced. <u>Always double-space</u>. No exceptions. That's the way it's done. It's easier for the editor to read, and it's easier for the editor to make changes. (Which is why that's the way it's done.)

<u>Use an easily-readable font</u>. This is not the time to show how clever and creative you can be with graphic design. Using what you feel is an elegant font, that you think enhances your article, will probably just make it harder to read. (And it doesn't enhance the article - it enhances the <u>appearance</u> of the article. And for a busy editor, with a stack of manuscripts to read, it doesn't even do that.)

The standard fonts are:

Times New Roman	(12 pt.)
Arial	(11 pt.)
Courier	(11 pt.)

You can use other fonts, but if you do, choose one that's easy to read, in a point size that will help - not hinder - the reader.

Hit your word count. If you've been asked for 2,000 words, turn in at least 2,000 words. That's part of your part of the deal. You can go over the count, but don't do it by very much. If your word count is 2,000 words, don't go over by more than 200 words or so.

When I say this in a workshop, often someone will ask, "Does that mean there's a 10% margin?" Not really. Because if you're doing a longer article, say, 4,000 words, then 10% would put you at 400 words over, and that's almost two pages. I use 200 words as a ceiling because that's about as much as you can write without adding an entire page to your manuscript. (And if you're assigned a smaller article, say 1,000 words, or 750 words, you shouldn't go over by that much.) The best thing, of course, is to come in right at your word count.

You don't have to name the article. Most magazines don't want you to. They have people on staff to do that. (However, sometimes an editor might want you to name the article, or suggest a name for it.)

You don't have to put the word count on every page. You don't have to put your name, address, and phone number on every page. (Unless you're told to, by the editor or the magazine's guidelines.)

When you're ready to turn in the finished article, you don't have to send it to the editor overnight priority special-delivery ultra-rush express. (Unless you've let that deadline get past you.) But, if you've managed your time right, you can just mail it, first-class mail.

With electronic communication increasingly becoming the norm, more and more editors are having writers send in articles via e-mail. Your editor might have already told you, during the phone call when you got the assignment, how she wanted you to send the article. If she has, do what she's asked you to do. But in that conversation some details might slip through the cracks, and this is often one that does.

When I'm ready to turn in a completed article, here's what I do...

Let's say my deadline is March 30. I will have that article absolutely finished, put to bed, ready to go, by March 25 (if not sooner). I've still got a good five days before the article is due.

I call the editor and let him know the article is finished. If we haven't worked out how he wants me to send it, we'll determine that now. The reason I'm calling five days before my deadline is, I want that article on his desk <u>by</u> the deadline. If he tells me to send it by regular mail, I have to allow a few days for it to reach him. If he wants me to send it electronically, there may be some details or glitches to work out. Electronic communication can sometimes get complicated, especially when working across platforms.

After this conversation, I send the article. If I've worked with the magazine before, I'll send my invoice with the article. If I haven't worked with the magazine before, I'll wait to send my invoice. (You'll find a sample invoice on page 141.)

Always put an invoice number on your invoice. It helps the accounting department, it helps you track your invoices, and it looks more professional.

The invoice on page 141 has what appears to be the name of the article. It's not. This apparent-title is for identification purposes. It's a way to refer to the article. Maybe I'm doing more than one piece for this magazine. Maybe they have another writer whose name is similar to mine. Maybe this editor is dealing with several writers, and keeps getting us all confused. Launching a second career is what this article is about, so that's a handy way to refer to it.

If the magazine pays expenses, include your expenses on the invoice, broken out by category. They'll want receipts. Send copies, in case the originals get lost. (And be sure you have additional copies of your receipts.) On page 143 you'll find an invoice that includes expenses.

My deadline is March 30. I send the article on March 25. On April 1, I call the editor again to make sure he's received the article. Not to ask if he's read it - he hasn't. I just to want be sure it got there when it was supposed to get there.

Don't ask the editor if he likes the piece. He hasn't read it yet. If he has read it, and has something to say, he'll say it.

After two to three weeks, if I haven't heard from the editor, I call one more time to tie up any loose ends.

By now he probably has read the piece. But don't expect him to sing your praises with compliments like, "Wow! Are you a good writer!"

Sometimes editors will be free with praise. Other times all you'll get is a quick, casual "Yeah, it looks fine." If you're looking for ego strokes, this isn't the place. Editors aren't there to stroke your ego. Your reward is they're paying you and publishing your writing.

That doesn't mean you'll never get compliments on your work. But remember that your editor is also dealing with other (perhaps all the other) articles in that issue of the magazine, as well as articles from several other issues.

If you haven't been told when they're publishing your piece, find out now.

If I haven't sent my invoice yet, I'll send it after this call. Because, assuming the editor has read the piece, and assuming there aren't any problems with it, his quick, casual "Yeah, it looks fine" means that the article has been accepted. If I'm being paid on acceptance, the payment process can now begin (and the first part of that process is my sending the magazine an invoice). If I'm being paid on publication, I won't get my money until the article is published, but they've still got to have an invoice. Once the article is accepted (regardless of how I'm paid or when they actually publish it), this job is done. I want my invoice in, so it's one less thing I have to keep track of.

What happens next between you and this editor?
Often nothing.

Even under the best of circumstances, this could be the last time you'll hear from him. Many editors will say the next time you have an idea you think is right for the magazine, give them a call. Some editors may say, "Nice work! What else do you have for us?" Even better, an editor might say, "Really good piece. Want another assignment?" These are all wonderful developments. (Especially that last one!) You're on your way to building a relationship with that magazine.

More often, however, you'll have to query the magazine again, the same way you did the first time. Of course, this time you have an advantage: your relationship with an editor.

If you do pitch this magazine again, send your query to "your" editor. And the letter can be more informal. (If the magazine has different editors for different sections, and your next idea is a match for one of these sections, send your query to the editor of that section, not the editor you've just worked with. But mention that you've done an article for this magazine, and mention the editor you worked with.)

Even with a relationship, there's no guarantee your next pitch to that magazine will be successful. In fact, aside from the fact that they've worked with you, and know you, and know your work, your chances of getting the assignment are the same as before you worked with them. You've still got to have an idea they can use, it still has to be timely, you still have to present it well, and you're still competing with all the other writers querying this magazine. Yes, you have an advantage over writers who've never been published here... But you've still got to come up with the goods.

And this has nothing to do with you - as a person or as a writer.

GETTING PUBLISHED...

You know when the issue of the magazine with your piece in it is coming out. Your editor has told you, probably when she called to give you the assignment. If for any reason you haven't been told, you've asked during your last phone call to the editor.

When the magazine hits the newsstands, go out and buy it. (No, they don't send you free copies.)

About being published...

What you write isn't always what appears in print.

Although it will appear under your name. In magazine work, you're a hired gun. They have the right (and they will not hesitate) to change your writing. For any reason whatsoever.

Sometimes they improve your writing. Sometimes they muck it up. Sometimes they muck it up really badly. And it's still published under your name.

I've had articles published word-for-word as I wrote them. I've had articles published with only a paragraph changed, usually taken out. (Unfortunately, it was always a very important paragraph.) Once I had an article published that was changed so much (and so much for the worse) that I wanted my name off it. (And the fact that this has happened to me only once makes me one very lucky writer.)

But... Whether you like what appears in print, or don't like what appears in print... The important thing is, you are now a published writer.

You have writing samples. Clips...tear sheets...tears...

And here's what you do:

Break down a copy of the magazine. If it's center-stapled, I remove the staples. If it's glue-bound, I neatly cut out the pages with a razor.

Include every page on which your article appears. Include any graphics (photographs, illustrations). No, you didn't do those, but it gives your sample a more finished, more professional look.

Most magazines print their name and the publication date (month, year) on each page or each two-page spread. Be sure this information appears on your samples.

Using a high-quality copy machine, make lots of photocopies. (If there are graphics or pictures involved, use the photographic setting on the copy machine.)

Black-and-white copies will do just fine. You generally do not get samples back (so there's no reason to go to the extra expense of color copies), and you're sending your writing, which is text, so there's no reason to make color copies so the graphics will look better.

These are your samples. This is what you send people when they ask for writing samples, or clips. And when you send writing samples, never send originals. You don't get samples back.

Congratulations! You've been published.

And the cycle starts all over again.

So... Got any good ideas?

QUESTIONS...

How many ideas should I be putting out there at once?

That depends on you... How you work, how you prefer to work, and how you may have to work. I like to do one piece at a time, and get in to that piece up to my elbows. So I send out one idea at a time. (That's once I get an assignment. When I'm pitching, I'll send out as many ideas as I have.) Other writers like to have a lot of balls in the air, enjoy working on several things at once, or have to work on several things at once so they have enough money coming in.

But...be careful about taking on more than you can handle. If you have so much going on that the quality of your work is affected, you should take a look at what you may be doing wrong, or think about how you can be doing it all better.

If I wait until I finish an article to send out my next query, won't there be a lot of downtime between pieces?

Yes. One thing I don't like about freelancing is that just when you're finishing up an article, and you want to be feeling good about that, perhaps relax a little, you have to be thinking about, and laying the groundwork for, your next piece.

If you get multiple assignments, this isn't an issue. But if, like me, you prefer to work on one thing at a time, there will be downtime between assignments. (Unless you've pitched a new idea when you hit the mid-point of your last assignment, and a new job begins before or as the current job ends.)

The key here is time management and pacing - managing your time, and pacing yourself, so you generate a steady flow of work. (If you <u>can</u> generate a steady flow of work. Just because you send out queries, doesn't mean you're going to get assignments.)

If an editor never gets back to me about my query, shouldn't I just assume they're not interested and move on to the next magazine?

Yes and no. An editor who doesn't get back to you probably isn't interested - or he'd get back to you. But he might not be getting back to you simply because he hasn't gotten to your query.

If an editor doesn't get back to me after I send Letter #6, I assume he's not interested and I do move on. But until you get that rejection letter, there's always the possibility they are interested. Until you get a rejection, there's always the chance you'll get an acceptance. With that in mind, I keep contacting a magazine until I get a rejection.

But I send Letter #6 only once. After I've sent Letter #6, and given an editor a deadline, if I send another follow-up letter I go back to Letter #5. Having given that editor one deadline, I'm not going to give him another every time I send him a follow-up letter about the same query. If I give a new deadline with each letter, the deadline doesn't mean very much.

Also, after the deadline I set in Letter #6 comes and goes, I start sending that idea to other magazines. If I send several follow-up letters to the same editor, and he doesn't get back to me until the fourth follow-up letter, by then I may be working on that article for a different magazine. But if I've set a new deadline with each follow-up letter, the latest deadline may not have arrived. In which case I'm (apparently) violating my own terms by not waiting for the last deadline before sending the query to another magazine. So when you give an editor a deadline, do it only once.

*How do I know when to give up on an idea
that I haven't sold?*

You don't.

And, you do: When you want to give up.

Again, until you get that rejection letter, there's always the possibility of a sale. Sometimes it takes years to sell that perfect idea that just can't miss. (I had a perfect idea that just couldn't miss three years ago. I still haven't sold it.)

All it takes for an idea to hit is one editor who can use it when you send it to her. So even if you've gotten 30 rejections on an idea, there's the possibility that query #31 will be the one that sells.

Which is why you keep putting that idea out there.

Unless you just get tired of hawking the same idea...it's no longer timely or relevant...or there are other things you want to move on to.

Should I send writing samples with my query letter?

My gut response is, No. Because sending samples, unasked for, is the sign of a new writer.

Now, one of the first things I said in this book is, there's nothing wrong with being a new writer. And that's so true, and so important to remember, that I'll repeat it: There is nothing wrong with being a new writer.

But neither is there much to be gained from advertising it. Which is why I take the position that, since sending samples unasked for is the sign of a new writer, don't do it.

I said that to a friend who was trying to break in to magazines. She immediately responded, "Well that's fine for you. But I _am_ a new writer. I need all the help I can get!"

And she was absolutely right.

So... If you feel that sending samples with your query letter will in any way help you... If it will give you more confidence, make you feel more secure, help make the editor want to give you the assignment... In any way give you any sort of edge... Then Do It.

The purpose of the query letter is to get you the assignment. And anything that does that, or helps do it, is an OK thing to do.

(And, lest I sound cavalier about writing samples... I may not send samples unasked for, but I _always_ let people know I _have_ samples, and will be more than happy to send them, on request.)

One more thought about sending samples...

If a magazine's guidelines indicate you should send samples with your query, and you're a new writer who has samples, it may speed things up if you do send samples with your proposal. Because what could happen is, the editor likes your query, but, because you're a new writer, she wants to see samples before she gives you the assignment. If she already has your samples, she doesn't have to contact you to ask for them (and you don't have to send them separately), and she can make her decision faster.

What happens if I get published but I'm not happy
with the article because it's been changed?
What do I do with samples like that?

A common problem. You get published, you have a writing sample, but you're unhappy with what was published. What do you do?

The quick, easy answer is, you don't use that sample. The problem with that answer is, you have that option, that luxury, only if you've been published several times. New writers generally don't have lots of samples to pick and choose among.

Even when you do have lots of samples, you still don't always have this luxury. I have published pieces I'm extremely unhappy with. And sometimes they happen to be the most relevant writing I have to show, given the idea I'm pitching or the project I'm going out for.

And if you send an editor a sample you don't like, you can't say to that editor, "An editor mucked this up."

When I have so send writing samples I'm unhappy with, I say in my cover letter something like, "What I wrote isn't exactly what was published. I'll be happy to send you the original material if you'd like to see it."

This tells the person on the other end that I'm aware this writing sample isn't very good, and that it's not my fault it's not very good. And lets them know I have an alternative version (that I feel better about and am willing to take responsibility for).

But when you're grappling with a writing sample you're unhappy about, keep this in mind: Just because you don't like it, doesn't mean an editor will have a problem with it.

If I have photographs of what I want to write about, should I include them with the query?

That depends on several things. First and foremost, are your photographs good? Are they good enough to be published? If they aren't, do not include them with your query. What the editor will see is less-than-adequate photography work, and you'll be risking that perception extending to your writing. If the editor looks at the pictures first, and doesn't like them or can't use them because they're not good photographs, and then she reads your query, her negative response to your pictures could easily carry over and influence her response to your query. Whether she's conscious of this or not. You're also risking the perception that <u>all</u> your work is less than adequate.

Another consideration is, are you pitching a high-end, or mid-range (or low-end) magazine? High-end magazines have their own photographers cover a story. Which is just as well. You're a writer, not a photographer, and you want the editor to perceive you as a writer. (Unless you <u>are</u> a photographer as well as a writer. But even so, most high-end magazines will want to work with photographers they know. If you are both a photographer and a writer, you might try this: let the editor get to know you as a writer. Then, when she sees what you can do in that area, let her know you're also a photographer and introduce her to your photographic work. If she likes what she sees, new opportunities might open up for you at that magazine. But take it a step at a time.)

Some mid-range (and many low-end) magazines do use a writer's pictures to illustrate that writer's article. (For which they pay you, in addition to your writing fee.) And with some low-end magazines, the fact that you have pictures can make the difference in getting the assignment. (You already have pictures (for which they'll pay you), so you're saving them the cost of a photographer.

If you have good (publishable) pictures, and you're pitching a magazine where this could make a difference, by all means include the pictures with your query. (But never your only copies.) And if for some reason you'd rather not include the pictures, let the editor know that you <u>have</u> pictures.

A magazine's policies (and pay rates) regarding photographs is included in its *Writer's Market* profile, and the magazine's writer's guidelines.

> *I know someone who did things you say not to do*
> *(like telephone an editor he didn't know),*
> *and everything worked out fine for him.*
> *How do you explain that?*

There are also people who sell their first screenplay for $1,000,000. And writers who leap off bridges because they've written 27 books that never got published.

Luck. Stuff happens. The permutations of any situation are endless.

For every person who breaks the rules and has wonderful things happen, there are countless people who break the rules and pay the price. Bad luck.

I know someone who called an editor she didn't know and had a lovely conversation with him. But she never did sell that article.

In the end, it comes down to doing what you're comfortable with.

I break my share of rules. Sometimes it works out for me. Sometimes it doesn't.

We make our choices, and we live with the results.

But consider this: If you're going to choose to break the rules, ignore the protocols, do it <u>your</u> way, all the time... And you notice it isn't working, or not working as well, or as much as you thought it would, or want it to be... Maybe there's a reason.

As I said in the Introduction...

I'm not saying I have all the answers. I'm not saying I do it perfectly, and my way is the only way to do it. Take from here what helps you, and use it well. Discard what you feel isn't helpful. Use the information in this book to find a better way.

And may you publish and prosper.

RIGHTS
WHAT ARE THEY BUYING...
WHAT ARE YOU SELLING?

ALL RIGHTS
The magazine buys all rights and owns the piece.
You cannot sell this article anywhere else. (You can write another article on the same topic and sell it to another magazine.)

FIRST SERIAL RIGHTS
The magazine buys the right to publish the article for the first time in a periodical publication. You keep all other rights to this article. (A variation of this is NORTH AMERICAN SERIAL RIGHTS. Some magazines buy these rights to publish first in the U.S. and Canada.)

SECOND SERIAL RIGHTS   (REPRINT RIGHTS)
The magazine buys the right to publish the article after it has appeared in another publication.
You get paid again for the exact same piece. Before you sell reprint rights, contact the magazine in which the article first appeared. Each magazine has its own policies regarding reprint rights.

ONE-TIME RIGHTS
The magazine buys the right to publish the article once. It has no guarantee that it will be the only - or the first - magazine to publish this article. You can sell the identical article to other publications. (Sometimes called simultaneous rights.)

JOHN GARRITY
1995 Market St.
San Francisco, California 94130
(415) 246-1357

INVOICE

7/15/02

INVOICE # 123

TO: Helen Maxwell

TODAY'S WOMAN

RE: Article

Launching A Second Career

AMOUNT DUE: $ 1, 000.

JOHN GARRITY
1995 Market St.
San Francisco, California 94130
(415) 246-1357

INVOICE

7/15/02

INVOICE # 123

TO: Helen Maxwell

TODAY'S WOMAN

RE: Article

Launching A Second Career	$	1,000.

Phone	$	27.35
Gas	$	10.00
Parking	$	5.00
Tolls	$	6.00
	$	48.35

AMOUNT DUE: $ 1, 048.35

SOME ADVICE FROM BOB THE ACCOUNTANT

As a freelance writer, you're an independent contractor. Which means (among other things) that no withholding tax is taken out of your income. It takes some freelancers years to figure out how to deal with this well. Until they do, they're surprised every April 15 because they owe taxes.

The best way to deal with this is to know your tax bracket (what percentage of your income you pay in taxes), deduct that amount from every check you receive (as a freelancer), set it aside, and don't touch it for any reason whatsoever except to pay taxes.

Remember to set aside money for state taxes as well as federal taxes.

If you're self-employed, you have to pay estimated taxes every quarter.

If you set aside the right amount of money every time you get a check, and make your estimated tax payments (on time, and correctly), taxes should pretty much take care of themselves.

Some magazines send separate checks for your writing fee and expenses. Some magazines send one check for both the writing fee and expenses.

Later, when they send you a 1099, you'll find your writing fees and expenses listed as one figure, and it's all income. A little unfair, since the expenses never were income.

When you do your taxes, remember to include those expenses in your deductions.

RESOURCES...

FINDING WRITER'S GUIDELINES ONLINE

I'm not saying these are the only Web sites that have writer's guidelines. I'm not saying they're the best sites. What works (or doesn't work) for me, might not work (or work) for you. And everyone has different needs. You can always go to Yahoo, Google, Alta Vista, or your search engine of choice, do an advanced search for writer's guidelines, and see what you can find. You might discover the perfect Web site for your needs.

WritersMarket.com.

Lists many publications, but to see them all (or an entire listing), you have to subscribe (annual service: $29.99, with a 30-day money-back guarantee. Or you can pay $2.99 a month, and cancel at any time).

worldwidefreelance.com

On this site you have to select publications by continent. You then get an alphabetical list of publications, and have to click on each title individually. Sometimes you get guidelines, sometimes you get links to the guidelines on the magazine's Web site.

writerswrite.com

Guidelines are listed alphabetically by magazine title, accessible by clicking on a link. There are also links to magazines' Web sites.

FILING COMPLAINTS...
AVOIDING PROBLEMS...

When you deal with established magazines, that have been around for a while, things generally go smoothly and (hopefully) there will be few, if any, problems.

When you deal with what could be called "fringe" markets (new low-end magazines...start-ups...and be <u>very</u> careful about anything connected with the Internet), it's a good idea to check out a prospective employer before you do the work. It also helps to have a way of taking action if problems develop later.

Here are some Web sites that can help you do both. On all three sites you can file a complaint or post a problem. You can also see if other writers have complaints about or had problems with a person, publication, or company.

And, again: Everyone has different needs. You can always go to Yahoo, Google, Alta Vista, or your search engine of choice, do an advanced search for "Writers" or "Writing," and see what you can find. You might discover the perfect Web site for your needs.

WritersWeekly.com

A Web site for writers, and an excellent resource. Has a Warnings section that lists complaints and bad experiences writers have had with people, publications, and companies. The list is constantly growing (which means it's current), arranged alphabetically, and includes the original complaint as well as what (if anything) has happened since the complaint was posted.

This Web site also lists magazines open to freelance submissions, and has magazine profiles similar to those in *Writer's Market*.

absolutewrite.com

A Web site for writers. Click on The Absolute Writer Water Cooler...scroll down to The Conference Room...click on The Bewares Board. This is a message board where writers post questions, problems, complaints, scam alerts, etc. Click on a message and you'll see responses.

bbb.org

This is the Better Business Bureau's Web site. You can see if complaints have been filed against the company or person you're considering doing business with. Organized by state.

Printed in the United States
15671LVS00001B/350